CLARITY

CONFIDENCE

EFFECTIVENESS

VITALITY

The Fit Leader's Companion

A Down-to-Earth Guide
for Sustainable Leadership Success

By Dr. David Chinsky

INSTITUTE *for*
LEADERSHIP FITNESS®

Printed in the USA

This publication is meant to strengthen your common sense, not substitute for it. It is also not a substitute for the advice of your doctor, lawyer, accountant, or any of your advisors, personal or professional.

SECOND EDITION

Edited by Amy Bell
Designed by CiesaDesign

ISBN 978-0-9835335-2-8

Praise for
The Fit Leader's Companion

Dr. David Chinsky has created the ideal methodology for individuals to develop and maintain the competencies of leadership. The Fit Leader's Companion is the best self development book since Dr. Stephen Covey's The Seven Habits of Highly Effective People.

My Company has used Dr. Chinsky's leadership fitness methodology exclusively for the past four years, and let me tell you...IT WORKS! Since employing his techniques of clarity, confidence, effectiveness and vitality, the company has experienced extraordinary results including: top line growth; strong profitability; and consistently rated as one of the best places to work.

Please read, enjoy and live The Fit Leader's Companion!

— Elliot Forsyth
Senior Vice President, Human Resources
ProQuest LLC

The Fit Leader's Companion goes well beyond traditional leadership books, and serves as a road map for not only meeting personal and professional goals, but living deeply meaningful and rewarding lives.

As an HR leader and professional, I can attest first-hand that most organizations pay little to no attention to the vitality of their leaders, and fail to recognize our collective quest to live productive, meaningful and fulfilling lives inside and outside of work. The underlying message of wellness as a characteristic of Fit Leaders is an emerging trend that insightful organizations will recognize and embrace.

The Fit Leader's Companion represents David's well-researched and personal views of what it takes to be a highly successful leader. I know David to be an authentic and genuine coach, an accomplished leader and author who offers highly pragmatic tips and solutions for living life on our own terms.

— Deborah Young
Vice President, Human Resources – North America
R.L. Polk & Company

David Chinsky has distilled 25 years of professional success and an abundance of wisdom to create The Fit Leader's Companion. The result: an easily absorbed framework which will powerfully serve leaders smart enough to heed its teachings. The reader who embraces the practical advice offered in this book can expect a noticeable and immediate uptick in leadership effectiveness.

— Julie K. Norris
Director of Attorney Development
Honigman Miller Schwartz and Cohn LLP

David has a keen focus on the highly-complex and often ambiguous dynamic of "leadership" and has succeeded in crafting an elegant, relevant and intuitive approach for readers to learn and implement his ground-breaking Leadership Fitness model.

— Steven Stralser, Ph.D.
Clinical Professor of Entrepreneurship & Innovation,
Thunderbird School of Global Management
Author, *MBA in a DAY—What you would learn at Top Tier Business Schools (if you only had the time!)*

If Cliffs Notes are the fastest way to help students learn, then The Fit Leader's Companion is the best surrogate any executive will find in quickly learning how to excel as a leader. Chinsky's recipe for leadership fitness includes all the right ingredients that result in a perfectly balanced, easy to use companion that every leader should devour.

— Carol Diephuis
President, Robranna LLC

The author's Leadership Fitness program is a practical and progressive foundation for renewed leadership in any organization. The Fit Leader's Companion is a refreshing and very pragmatic approach that summarizes David Chinsky's profound experience and passion for innovative leadership.

— Otto Siegel, MCC
Genius Coach and co-author of *Yes, You Are a Genius – Whether You Know it or Not*

I found The Fit Leader's Companion full of information I have already begun to use. Finally, a book that is simple but not simplistic and a model of leadership that doesn't overlook the importance of personal vitality.

— Chris Johnson
Founder, On Target Living International

David's passion for leadership shines throughout The Fit Leader's Companion. This inventive approach to leadership is replete with sensible and straightforward principles. He has created a compelling and powerful teaching instrument for the individual who strives for Sustainable Leadership. Having known David for 10 years, he is exemplary of the role Vitality plays for an effective leader.

— Todd E. Breault
Director of Sales, Evana Automation

There are lots of books on theories of leadership, but what makes this one unique and so powerful is David's 25 years of personal experience both as a CEO and a Leadership Coach to over 1,000 leaders, managers and owners of companies. This real world experience is seen in every chapter, and the exercises alone are worth their weight in gold! I highly recommend this book and I'll be first in line to buy it!

— Stephen Fairley
CEO, The Rainmaker Institute, LLC

Dedication

I dedicate this book to the thousands of people who

lost their lives on September 11, 2001.

Through an ironic twist of fate, it was the tragedy on "9/11"

that ultimately liberated me to realize my dream of starting

a leadership development practice of my own.

Table of Contents

Part I. Clarity: The First Face of Leadership Fitness

Part II. Confidence: The Second Face of Leadership Fitness

Part III. Effectiveness: The Third Face of Leadership Fitness

Part IV. Vitality: The Fourth Face of Leadership Fitness

Exercise Worksheets

About The Fit Leader's Program™

Acknowledgements

This book is the result of half a lifetime of experiences. During the early part of my career, I had the privilege of leading and learning from thousands of people in a handful of companies, including Trinity Health, Ford Motor Company, Nestle and Thomson Reuters.

I've had the good fortune of being led by a handful of very able executive leaders from whom I learned much. I acknowledge these leaders who believed in me and who supported my own development as an aspiring leader and manager: Michael Madden, the late LeRoy Fahle, Jack Shelton, Tom Kilarski, Powell Woods, Ernest Ludy, Larry Hagerty and J. Dennis Bush.

I also wish to thank all of the leaders, and their various sponsors, that have enrolled in our Fit Leader's Program™ and Fit Leaders Academy since 2008. I have gained much from the experience of working with them in our programs, and I appreciate their ongoing support as I focus on my bold mission of training 10,000 fit leaders.

I also wish to thank my first leaders in life, the late Edward and Rochelle Chinsky, who taught me that I could accomplish anything I set my sights on. There is no greater gift than the unconditional love of one's parents. I am forever grateful to them for the opportunities they gave to me, and for the solid values they taught and demonstrated each day of their lives.

Last, and certainly not least, I wish to acknowledge the wonderful life I have been blessed to live with Eva, my partner of over 40 years, and our two grown children, Joel and Clara. Eva's love and support through the years has created the only security I've ever felt I needed in this life. Joel and Clara remind me each day of the importance of leaving a legacy, and inspire me to continue to seek ways to contribute and make meaning in the world.

INTRODUCTION

The Four Faces of Leadership Fitness®

Over the years, I have asked thousands of participants in my leadership workshops an important question: How do you define the key activities of leadership? Many participants answer that a successful leader is the primary visionary for the organization, while others point to leaders as motivators, risk takers and delegators. Still others view leaders as masterful communicators, reflective thinkers and energetic forces who have the power to drive their organizations forward.

As a leadership coach, I develop agile, competent and energetic leaders. Throughout my coaching career, I have discovered that fit leaders possess four common threads that weave together to form 40 essential leadership traits. I call these four threads the Four Faces of Leadership Fitness. In the following chapters, I will explain these four common threads and the 40 primary leadership traits in greater detail.

But first, let me introduce my Leadership Fitness® model. This model illustrates how fit leaders create impact and obtain success by developing clarity, confidence, effectiveness and vitality.

What is Leadership Fitness?

Leadership Fitness is an integrated model of leadership development. I created this model based on my 20+ years of personal leadership experience and over 20 years of professionally coaching and training high-potential leaders.

After spending many years working with promising leaders, a colleague suggested that I document my philosophy on developing leadership talent. This was an excellent suggestion because it forced me to really think about what I was doing in my practice to create sustainable success for the individuals and the organizations I had the privilege to serve.

As I embarked on this process of defining a unique approach to developing leaders, something incredible happened—a handful of very specific leadership foundations surfaced. I identified four crucial components of leadership success that create long-term impact for leaders and their organizations: clarity, confidence, effectiveness and vitality. When leaders consistently demonstrate all four of these leadership qualities, I call them "fit leaders."

A Down-to-Earth Guide for Sustainable Leadership Success
1

Clarity: The First Face of Leadership Fitness

The first component that emerged in the leadership fitness model was clarity. Based on my work with leaders and their teams, I observed that successful leaders knew how to set a clear direction and articulate a compelling vision that encouraged their people to follow their lead.

More than anything else, employees seek clarity from their leaders. Leaders who lack clarity or who do not take the time to provide clear direction create an unstable environment where team members are forced to choose from multiple priorities. This often results in employees saying or thinking things like, "We don't know where we are going," or "I'm not sure what I am supposed to be working on."

Confidence: The Second Face of Leadership Fitness

As I continued working on the model, I identified confidence as the second face of leadership fitness. While clarity creates an essential strong foundation for action, I discovered the most successful leaders combine their sense of direction with a powerful self-confidence that amplifies their message. Employees have a keen sixth sense, a sort of radar, when it comes to interpreting what they hear from their leaders. Even if a leader's words are logical and understandable, employees will notice if there is a lack of authenticity. If a team senses that the leader does not truly believe in what he is saying, his message is quickly compromised.

Professionals use a variety of words to describe those powerful inner voices that create self-doubt. Some call them "gremlins" while others refer to them as "saboteurs." Regardless of how we label them, these internal doubts often diminish our overall impact by causing us to second guess our beliefs and intentions. Fit leaders learn how to quiet these harmful inner voices and develop strategies to effectively push ahead with conviction and self-assurance. Fit leaders also have the resiliency to win over their employees.

Effectiveness: The Third Face of Leadership Fitness

As I delved deeper into my experiences, I pinpointed the third leadership fitness component: effectiveness. The most successful leaders possess a host of execution and implementation skills necessary to give life to their bold visions. In other words, fit leaders are effective. Fit leaders are effective because they know how to:

- Delegate authority
- Promote healthy conflict
- Provide feedback at the teachable moment
- Build accountable teams
- Facilitate successful transitions
- Develop other leaders

I have coached and trained many executives possessing large doses of clarity and confidence—but they lacked the effectiveness to get anything done. The focus on effectiveness is all about creating accountability and driving sustainability for the leader's organization.

Vitality: The Fourth Face of Leadership Fitness

Once I identified clarity, confidence and effectiveness as crucial contributors to leadership fitness, I thought the model was complete. I asked myself, "If I can help an organization develop clear, confident and effective leaders, what else could they possibly want?"

Then I realized that I had been asked to coach and train many leaders who were clear, confident and effective...yet they still failed to go the distance. Even though these leaders had a clear direction for their teams, the ability to tame their inner voices or gremlins and a complete set of effectiveness tools, they were still growing frustrated, overwhelmed and even physically ill. Why? Because they weren't attending to their own health and vibrancy. As a result, these leaders were unable to sustain their influence because they ran out of steam.

Recognizing this limitation, I decided to add one last component to the model: vitality. I see vitality as a measure of our energy, stamina and endurance. With this powerful addition, leaders can manage the numerous and competing demands for their time and remain engaged for the long haul.

When my work was complete, I had created an integrated model of leadership fitness comprising four major components: clarity, confidence, effectiveness and vitality. I will expound upon each of these four components in the following four sections of this book.

In each chapter, I will also provide a true story to clearly demonstrate these leadership concepts and show how they apply "In the Real World." These examples are based on my own experiences as well as actual events I have witnessed and conversations I have had throughout my professional career. I hope these stories will offer you a solid understanding of each concept and, in some cases, provide a little bit of comic relief.

Are you ready to transform into a fit leader with the clarity, confidence, effectiveness and vitality you need to drive your organization to the next level? *Let's get started!*

PART 1

CLARITY:

The First Face of Leadership Fitness

CLARITY

An Introduction

Fit leaders always establish and communicate a clear sense of direction. The most successful leaders can assess the reality of a current situation, often with brutal honesty, and then chart a new course for moving entire teams from "where we are today" to "where we need to be tomorrow."

More than anything else, employees seek clarity from their leaders. When a leader lacks clarity or simply does not take the time to provide clear direction to his team, employees are forced to choose from multiple priorities. Without clear direction, employees remain unsure of what they should be working on or where the team is headed.

Obviously, it is extremely difficult to lead in this kind of confusing atmosphere. It is also terribly distracting for employees who are trying to figure out where to focus their time and energy. Even worse, a leader who cannot offer clarity will quickly lose credibility. When employees look to their leaders for direction and it is not there, they begin to wonder who (if anyone) is steering the ship.

If you want to bring clarity to your team, you'll have to ask some hard questions about your organization's core purpose and priorities:

- What expectations do I have for my staff and how can I share these expectations with them?

- How can I remove ambiguity and more clearly communicate with my team?

- How can I find time to reflect on my goals and work *on* my business—not just *in* it?

- What keeps my customers up at night and what matters most to them?

1) Set Clear Expectations 2) Remove Ambiguity 3) Take Time for Reflection 4) Know What Keeps Your Customers Up at Night
5) Stay Focused 6) Ask Open-Ended Questions 7) Make Time for Meaningful Conversations 8) Round Regularly
9) Articulate Your Mission, Vision and Values 10) Sort and Prioritize Opportunities Competing for Your Attention

- How can I stay focused on my objectives and develop true conviction?

- What powerful questions can I ask my employees to promote productive conversations?

- What can I gain by having meaningful, one-on-one conversations with my team members?

- What can I do to become more visible and accessible to my staff?

- How can I clearly define my organization's mission, vision and values and share this information with my team?

- How can I sort through and prioritize the opportunities that compete for my attention?

In the following ten chapters, I will help you answer each of these questions and discuss how you can create clarity, the first face of leadership fitness. However, it's important to understand that you cannot reach the highest level of leadership fitness through clarity alone. You will also need to develop confidence, effectiveness and vitality. Clarity is simply the first step on this journey.

CHAPTER

1

Set Clear Expectations

Fit leaders know how to set clear expectations for their teams. If your employees do not understand what you expect of them, they will quickly lose focus. They will simply wander about without a sense of purpose or direction, and you will never reach your goals as a team.

If you want to set concrete expectations for your team, first determine what is essential for your organization to succeed. Only then can you pinpoint the expectations you have for your employees—the behaviors and actions that will propel your organization towards success.

Once you nail down this list of expectations, take time to discuss them with your staff. Consider giving each employee a written copy of your expectations or posting the list in a high-traffic area, such as the break room or conference room. Sit down with your staff and review your list of expectations several times a year to ensure that everyone is clear about what matters most to your organization.

Are you setting clear expectations for your team? Ask yourself the following questions:

SETTING EXPECTATIONS EXERCISE

- What behaviors and actions do you expect of your team?

- How well does your team understand what is expected of them?

- How can you more clearly define your expectations for your employees?

- How much time have you spent communicating your expectations to your staff?

- How could providing a written list of expectations to your team help them stay on track?

See page 140 for exercise worksheet.

1) Set Clear Expectations 2) Remove Ambiguity 3) Take Time for Reflection 4) Know What Keeps Your Customers Up at Night
5) Stay Focused 6) Ask Open-Ended Questions 7) Make Time for Meaningful Conversations 8) Round Regularly
9) Articulate Your Mission, Vision and Values 10) Sort and Prioritize Opportunities Competing for Your Attention

IN THE REAL WORLD

Establishing Great Expectations

As a leader, it's important to set clear expectations for your team to help them focus their behaviors and actions. When I assumed the senior executive leadership role for one of my former employer's most important business functions, the first thing I did was determine what was most important for our success moving forward. I identified eight expectations I believed would contribute most to the changed perception we were trying to create.

I then took the time to discuss these expectations with my new staff, and I gave each team member a written copy of these eight expectations. I requested that they review the list regularly to ensure they were living up to our commitments on a daily basis.

You might be thinking I went too far by circulating a set of written expectations or that this action was a little too paternalistic. However, I can tell you with great confidence that most employees appreciate the clarity that comes from knowing what their leaders deem important. The alternative is that they simply remain unsure of what really matters, leaving them with an incomplete sense of purpose or direction.

For years after I shared my expectations with my team, I would often spot the original list posted on my employees' file cabinets, bulletin boards or cubicle walls as I walked through the department. It was obvious that my team found value in the written list, and some of them said they referred to it on a weekly or even daily basis. When it comes to sharing expectations, particularly information about how we want to portray ourselves or behave around our customers, there is no substitute for providing employees with a clearly written copy.

Once you set and communicate your expectations for your team, it's important to regularly reinforce these expectations. This list of expectations will also serve as your basis for managing and enhancing staff performance. Hold each member of the team accountable for complying with the expectations.

Of course, accountability and clear expectations are closely linked. After all, you cannot hold someone accountable for their actions if they do not understand what is expected of them. This is precisely why you need to periodically review your expectations with your team to ensure that they consistently understand what you expect of them.

CHAPTER
2

Remove Ambiguity

When you communicate with your team, it is crucial to make sure they fully understand your message. How many times have you thought to yourself, "Why don't they get it? I've said it five times, and they *still* aren't doing what I asked them to do." Oftentimes, we are so clear in our own minds about what we are asking or saying that we actually leave out important information as we communicate it to others.

If you want to be a fit leader, you have to remove ambiguity from your conversations. Unfortunately, there are countless distractions and other forms of "static" that can potentially interrupt your conversation with an employee. This is why it's so important to communicate as clearly as possible and verify that the listener receives your message, loud and clear.

If you want to avoid ambiguity and master the art of crystal clear communications, ask yourself the following questions:

REMOVING AMBIGUITY EXERCISE

- How well does your team understand the direction you've set for the organization?

- What questions would you ask yourself to gain more clarity?

- How many times and how many different ways do you communicate an important message to your team?

- How much time and productivity have you lost in the past by being less than clear?

- What are the visible signs that others truly understand your message?

See page 141 for exercise worksheet.

1) Set Clear Expectations **2) Remove Ambiguity** 3) Take Time for Reflection 4) Know What Keeps Your Customers Up at Night
5) Stay Focused 6) Ask Open-Ended Questions 7) Make Time for Meaningful Conversations 8) Round Regularly
9) Articulate Your Mission, Vision and Values 10) Sort and Prioritize Opportunities Competing for Your Attention

IN THE REAL WORLD

Getting Rid of Communication Static

If you want to be a fit leader, it's critical to clearly communicate your messages and ensure those messages are actually heard and understood by others. In my dealings with employees and colleagues over the years, I've discovered a number of strategies leaders can employ to remove ambiguity or "static" from their communications.

After you communicate a point or give an assignment to an employee, you can simply ask, "What questions do you have for me?" Note that this is very different from asking, "Do you understand?" When you ask people if they understand, it is human nature for them to nod their heads in agreement. After all, most of us want to avoid any possible indication we in fact do *not* understand—or that perhaps we weren't listening.

This reminds me of an episode from the popular TV series *Seinfeld*. Jerry Seinfeld's friend George Costanza receives a job assignment from his boss, the manager of the New York Yankees. George is not paying attention and doesn't have a clue what his boss just asked him to do. Rather than admitting that he does not understand his assignment, George proceeds to spend all 30 minutes of the episode trying to figure out what his boss expects him to deliver. Of course, in typical Costanza fashion, George fails miserably to deliver the goods at the end of the show.

In a situation like George Costanza's, I don't know many leaders who wouldn't prefer their employees to simply raise their hand right then and there and say, "I'm sorry, but I just don't understand what you are asking me to do," or "I zoned out for a few seconds and I missed the last thing you said. Could you please repeat it?" This allows the manager to restate the assignment and fill in any missing information.

However, it's difficult for many people to admit that they were not listening or got distracted. That's why it's important for you to initiate questions to ensure you have accurately communicated the assignment and that your employee understands it. For example, you might ask, "How do you propose to proceed with this project?" or "What additional resources will you require?" or "What else can I share with you to help you get started?"

Most importantly, try to avoid ambiguity when you communicate with others. Make sure that nothing has interfered with your communication process and that your employee received the message loud and clear and static-free. If you want to double check that your employee understands, ask her to restate the assignment in her own words or summarize the assignment or discussion in writing. This gives you an opportunity to make sure both of you are on the same page, and it also gives you a chance to say, "That's not what I said," or "That's not what I meant. Let's go over this again."

Of course, it may take some extra time to ensure your employees understand your messages and assignments from the get-go. But trust me—it's well worth the investment. After all, you'll lose a lot more time in the end if the job doesn't get done, and you're left picking up the pieces. That's exactly what miscommunication and misunderstandings will get you.

1) Set Clear Expectations 2) Remove Ambiguity **3) Take Time for Reflection** 4) Know What Keeps Your Customers Up at Night
5) Stay Focused 6) Ask Open-Ended Questions 7) Make Time for Meaningful Conversations 8) Round Regularly
9) Articulate Your Mission, Vision and Values 10) Sort and Prioritize Opportunities Competing for Your Attention

CHAPTER
3

Take Time for Reflection

Fit leaders take time to think. They step back from the hustle and bustle of their daily business to meditate, ruminate and contemplate.

Fit leaders preserve the necessary space in their lives so they have room to evaluate alternatives and ponder the possibilities of their actions. Rather than prematurely rushing into action, leaders take time to study the big picture and consider their options. A fit leader allocates enough (but not too much) time to weigh the pros and cons of his plans.

Some leaders actually carve out a specific time on their calendars each day that is dedicated to reflection. Other leaders incorporate this important activity into their daily deliberations. Either way, if you want to be a fit leader, it's important to take time to reflect.

To become a more reflective leader, ask yourself the following questions:

REFLECTION EXERCISE

- How much time do you spend really pondering your possibilities?

- What processes do you employ to sufficiently consider alternatives?

- When have you caught yourself rushing to action prematurely?

- How much free space exists in your weekly schedule?

- How do you avoid analysis paralysis?

See page 142 for exercise worksheet.

Working *On* Your Business—Not Just *In* It

In an effort to be a more reflective leader, I spend one day each quarter really thinking about where my business is today and where it needs to go in the future. I started this practice after completing Dan Sullivan's highly-regarded program, The Strategic Coach®. For four days each year, I take time to focus on which big projects and key relationships I need to nurture in the next 90 days and figure out how to effectively execute my strategy.

By participating in this quarterly reflection process, I take the time to work *on* my business... not just *in* my business. Michael Gerber explains this important concept in his informative book, *The E-Myth Revisited: Why Most Small Businesses Don't Work and What to Do About It* (HarperCollins, 1995). Gerber points out that many business leaders spend too much time working *in* the business and not enough time working *on* the business.

If you want to be a reflective leader, take the time to ask yourself the right questions, contemplate your current position and determine whether or not you're still moving in the right direction.

I ask myself the following five questions each and every quarter:

- What big initiatives, projects or changes do I anticipate managing in the next 90 days?
- What relationships will I nurture or give time to during the next 90 days?
- What must I accomplish in the next 90 days to be satisfied with my progress, both personally and professionally?
- What gremlins will I tame during the next 90 days? What are some of the self doubts or some of the inner voices I'm hearing that I need to manage so they don't get in my way?
- What positive habits will feed my confidence during the next 90 days?

Not only do I personally follow this process, but I also encourage my clients in the Fit Leader's Program™ and Fit Leaders Academy to reflect on these questions every 90 days.

1) Set Clear Expectations 2) Remove Ambiguity 3) Take Time for Reflection **4) Know What Keeps Your Customers Up at Night**
5) Stay Focused 6) Ask Open-Ended Questions 7) Make Time for Meaningful Conversations 8) Round Regularly
9) Articulate Your Mission, Vision and Values 10) Sort and Prioritize Opportunities Competing for Your Attention

CHAPTER
4

Know What Keeps Your Customers Up at Night

Fit leaders know what matters most to their customers. They keep a finger on the pulse of their target market, stay connected with the clients they serve and pick up important signals from their customer base. Once a leader has a grasp on what keeps his customers up at night, he can effectively guide the organization's strategy.

A fit leader not only understands his customers' greatest concerns—he also knows what his clients need to succeed. He finds a way to offer relief for his customers' "pain points" and provide solutions to their problems. If you want to keep your organization relevant, you have to continually build and nurture relationships with those you serve.

In other words, go out and meet with your customers. There's really no substitute for getting in front of your customers on a regular basis. Sometimes, leaders feel like they know enough just from reading the trade press or having occasional phone conversations with their clients. But this is not enough. It is essential to visit with customers because these meetings will give you a better understanding of what your customers need and how you can give it to them.

If you want to stay connected with your customers, ask yourself the following questions:

UNDERSTANDING YOUR CUSTOMERS EXERCISE

- How much time are you spending with your key customers?

- What process does your organization use to share customer needs and concerns with the team members who need to know them?

- What are the top three business issues keeping your customers up at night?

- How does your organization track customer issues to create a sense of urgency around your company's agenda?

- How are you nurturing your key customer relationships?

See page 143 for exercise worksheet.

Meeting Face-to-Face with Customers

If you want to stay relevant in the marketplace, you need to understand the most serious issues your customers face. As I mentioned in this chapter, there is no substitute for getting in front of our customers on a regular basis. Although you may *think* you have a handle on your customers' needs, it is important to go out and actually visit with your customers to make sure you are right.

When I was General Manager for an Information Technology business, I made a practice of visiting each of my clients at least a couple of times a year. Not only did this let my customers know I was invested in their success—it also allowed me to get in front of them and see and hear what they were dealing with firsthand. The more I learned about their struggles, the more ways I could serve them.

There were many times when I was sitting in a client's office and happened to see something on his desk or overhear a conversation that led to an opportunity. I would suddenly realize, "This customer needs something my business can offer."

For example, during a casual lunch meeting with one of my clients, she revealed that her business had a serious need. She had never expressed this need to me because she thought it fell outside the normal scope of our work. But because I happened to be there talking with her and she mentioned the problem in passing, I was able to say, "It sounds like you've got a real issue there...and we can help." Of course, the client was thrilled, and she answered, "We would love your help!" That is why it's so important to get out and meet with your customers.

I always ask my clients in the Fit Leader's Program™, "What are the three biggest issues that keep your customers up at night?" For the most part, these leaders can recite at least three or more customer issues. So, at first glance, they seem to have a fair degree of understanding of their customers' needs.

However, as part of this exercise, I also encourage my students to go out and visit with their clients. I tell them to make sure there is alignment between the customers' actual problems and the solutions their business is providing. Once they go out and meet with their clients, these leaders often learn that their customers have more important problems that they are not addressing.

The moral of the story is this: If you want to genuinely understand your customers' needs and priorities, meet face-to-face with them.

1) Set Clear Expectations 2) Remove Ambiguity 3) Take Time for Reflection 4) Know What Keeps Your Customers Up at Night
5) Stay Focused 6) Ask Open-Ended Questions 7) Make Time for Meaningful Conversations 8) Round Regularly
9) Articulate Your Mission, Vision and Values 10) Sort and Prioritize Opportunities Competing for Your Attention

CHAPTER
5

Stay Focused

When faced with multiple choices, fit leaders trust in their instincts and training to make the right decision. In the end, a fit leader does what she believes is the right thing. Once a leader chooses a path, she remains confident about the direction she has chosen for the organization—and she does not take short cuts to achieving the end goal.

In other words, an effective leader stays focused on her objectives and desired outcomes. She consistently chooses courses of action that support the organization's overall strategies and intentions.

Of course, leaders cannot always remain on a straight path. The business world is unpredictable, and leaders often have to make mid-course corrections to adapt to the economy, industry shifts and other changes. When a fit leader realizes a change of direction is necessary, she moves quickly to adjust her course of action and gives little thought to selfishly protecting her initial positions.

To gain more focus, ask yourself the following questions:

FOCUS EXERCISE

- What must your team achieve in the next 90 days to move your strategy forward?

- What is currently distracting you from your focus on your objectives?

- What short-cuts are you tempted to take in an attempt to reach your goal more quickly?

- How tightly are you holding on to positions that no longer make sense or are no longer the best approach?

- What is the source of your clarity in the course you've charted?

See page 144 for exercise worksheet.

Finding the Balance
Between Conviction and Correction

Based on my own experiences, as well as my interactions with various leaders over the years, I have discovered that it is incredibly easy to stray from your intentions based on the last voice you hear. So, when a leader hears a contrary point of view, he may say, "Oh yeah, that sounds good. Maybe we should do it that way instead."

I believe that leaders often have a hard time staying focused because they do not possess the conviction they need from the beginning. As a result, they constantly waver on their position and habitually change course.

I have learned to inoculate myself from this kind of indecision by properly vetting my ideas before I set a direction. When I say leaders need to stay focused, I do not mean they should come up with their ideas in a vacuum and move forward without talking to others first. If you discuss your options with other experts and collect plenty of valuable input upfront, you'll move forward with more conviction. You will feel confident that you have considered all the alternatives and chosen the best course. Once you move forward, you'll be able to remain focused and stay on the right path.

However, when mid-course corrections are warranted, fit leaders know how to adapt quickly—instead of fighting to protect their initial positions. One of the examples I often use to illustrate this point is George W. Bush. President Bush had real conviction about moving forward in Iraq. Essentially, he led us into a war, and despite repeated pushback by opponents, he remained steadfast.

The president had the conviction that this was the right thing to do. He told us if we didn't take action, things would get worse—that in 10 years or 20 years, we'd look back and realize this was a good move. He didn't go back and forth. He made a decision, and he stuck with it. Of course, there were a lot of people who disagreed with his decision, yet he moved forward. I think it's a great example of a leader staying focused.

However, I think George W. Bush failed as a leader when it became clear that we needed to change course. He pretty much put on the blinders, and I think he fell prey to the selfish overprotecting of his initial position. He didn't have to say, "I made a mistake." He could have simply said, "Things have changed, and we need to change direction."

1) Set Clear Expectations 2) Remove Ambiguity 3) Take Time for Reflection 4) Know What Keeps Your Customers Up at Night
5) Stay Focused 6) Ask Open-Ended Questions 7) Make Time for Meaningful Conversations 8) Round Regularly
9) Articulate Your Mission, Vision and Values 10) Sort and Prioritize Opportunities Competing for Your Attention

On the one hand, I think President Bush is a great example of a leader who was steadfast and did not change his position every day based on poll numbers. Yet at some point, he had the opportunity to make a mid-course correction, and he failed to do so. So, I think he's a good example of both sides of the coin. He was elected president because the American people believed that he knew what we needed to do. He set a direction and he stuck to his guns. But then he failed to come back and say, "I think we need a new direction," which I think people also would have supported. As a result, we ended up mired in a very difficult situation, and we continue to pay a huge price.

CHAPTER

6

Ask Open-Ended Questions

Fit leaders establish clarity, in part, by asking their team members the right questions. If you want to invite your employees to share their best thoughts and ideas, it is crucial that you pay attention to the structure of your questions.

Whatever you do, try not to ask too many closed-ended questions—questions that can be answered with a simple "Yes" or "No." For example, "Have you completed the project?" or "Do you agree with this position?" These are both closed-ended questions. These types of narrow inquiries thwart meaningful conversations between you and your team.

Instead, ask your team members open-ended questions, which often begin with a "What" or a "How." For example, "What can we do to improve this process?" or "How should we go about targeting this group of customers?" When you ask these open-ended questions, you are inviting your employees to really think about their answers in a spirit of true discovery—instead of simply providing a one-word response.

Of course, it takes practice to replace your closed-ended questions with more powerful open-ended questions. If you want to be a fit leader, ask yourself the following open-ended questions:

OPEN-ENDED QUESTIONS EXERCISE

- How aware are you of the types of questions you ask every day?
- What is the risk of relying on closed-ended questions to get the information you seek?
- How can you replace closed-ended questions, that often serve as poorly disguised statements of your own position, with powerful open-ended questions?
- What would it be like to spend an entire meeting asking only open-ended questions?
- When is it appropriate to ask a closed-ended question?

See page 145 for exercise worksheet.

1) Set Clear Expectations 2) Remove Ambiguity 3) Take Time for Reflection 4) Know What Keeps Your Customers Up at Night
5) Stay Focused **6) Ask Open-Ended Questions** 7) Make Time for Meaningful Conversations 8) Round Regularly
9) Articulate Your Mission, Vision and Values 10) Sort and Prioritize Opportunities Competing for Your Attention

IN THE REAL WORLD

Asking Powerful Open-Ended Questions

Powerful questions are provocative queries that invite others to expand their horizons and consider fresh perspectives. When I was in training to become a professional certified coach, I came across a dynamic list of open-ended questions in *Co-Active Coaching: New Skills for Coaching People Toward Success in Work and Life* by Laura Whitworth, Henry Kimsey-House and Phil Sandahl (Davies-Black Publishing, 1998). For a long time, I kept this document next to my phone and often referred to it when I was meeting with a client or colleague. After a while, I began using these types of open-ended questions without even thinking about it. Here is a condensed version of the list:

ANTICIPATION	What might happen? What if it doesn't work out the way you wish? What if that doesn't work? And if that fails, what will you do? What is your backup plan?
ASSESSMENT	What do you make of it? What do you think is best? How does it look to you? How do you feel about it? What if it doesn't work out?
CLARIFICATION	What do you mean? What does it feel like? What seems to confuse you? What more can you say? What do you want?
FOR INSTANCE	If you could do it over again, what would you do differently? If it were you, what would you have done? How else could a person handle this? If you could do anything you wanted, what would you do? For instance?

HISTORY	What caused it? What led up to...? What have you tried so far? What do you remember most about how it happened? What do you make of it all?
IMPLEMENTATION	What is the action plan? What will you have to do to get the job done? What support do you need to accomplish...? What will you do? When will you do it?
INTEGRATION	What will you take away from this? How do you explain this to yourself? What was the lesson? How can you lock in the learning? How would you pull all this together?
OPTIONS	What are the possibilities? If you had your choice, what would you do? What are possible solutions? What if you do and what if you don't? What options can you create?
OUTCOMES	What do you want? What is your desired outcome? If you got it, what would you have? How will you know you have reached it? What would it look like?
PERSPECTIVE	When you are 95 years old, what will you want to say about your life? What will you think about this five years from now? How does this relate to your life purpose? In the bigger scheme of things how important is this? So what?
PLANNING	What do you plan to do about it? What is your game plan? What kind of plan do you need to create? How do you suppose you could improve the situation? Now what?

1) Set Clear Expectations 2) Remove Ambiguity 3) Take Time for Reflection 4) Know What Keeps Your Customers Up at Night
5) Stay Focused 6) Ask Open-Ended Questions 7) Make Time for Meaningful Conversations 8) Round Regularly
9) Articulate Your Mission, Vision and Values 10) Sort and Prioritize Opportunities Competing for Your Attention

PREDICTIONS	How do you suppose it will all work out? What will that get you? Where will this lead? What are the chances of success? What is your prediction?
RESOURCES	What resources do you need to help you decide? What do you know about it now? How do you suppose you can find out more about it? What kind of picture do you have right now? What resources are available to you?
SUBSTANCE	What seems to be the trouble? What seems to be the main obstacle? What is stopping you? What concerns you the most about…? What do you want?
SUMMARY	What is your conclusion? How is this working? How would you describe this? What do you think this all amounts to? How would you summarize the effort so far?
TAKING ACTION	What action will you take? And after that? What will you do? When? What is the best time to act? Where do you go from here? When will you do that? What are your next steps? By when?

CHAPTER

7

Make Time for Meaningful Conversations

We all struggle with packed calendars, rushed meetings and busy days. Fit leaders, however, find the time to carry on meaningful conversations with their employees and colleagues. If you don't proactively set time aside for these significant one-on-one conversations, you may end up going days, weeks and even months without connecting with your team members.

Unless you reach out to your employees, you'll never fully understand what is going on within your team and throughout your organization. So, if you don't slow down and connect with the team, your business will never pick up speed.

If you want to carry on more meaningful conversations, ask yourself the following questions:

MEANINGFUL CONVERSATIONS EXERCISE

- What are you doing today to create an environment of trust and mutual respect?

- How are you encouraging all members of your team to share their unique points of view?

- What is your practice around the use of electronic devices during one-on-one and group meetings?

- What impact would your commitment to having regular conversations have on overall employee engagement?

- How do you remain present when interacting with others?

See page 146 for exercise worksheet.

1) Set Clear Expectations 2) Remove Ambiguity 3) Take Time for Reflection 4) Know What Keeps Your Customers Up at Night
5) Stay Focused 6) Ask Open-Ended Questions **7) Make Time for Meaningful Conversations** 8) Round Regularly
9) Articulate Your Mission, Vision and Values 10) Sort and Prioritize Opportunities Competing for Your Attention

IN THE REAL WORLD

Six Steps to More Meaningful Conversations

Whether it's a colleague, employee, friend or family member, conversations are at the heart of every relationship. Our ability to build strong relationships with others, especially in the workplace, is inherently linked to our ability to have meaningful conversations. But what exactly constitutes a "meaningful conversation"? Meaningful conversations have depth. They connect individuals through common goals and values, and they reveal important issues that impact each individual and the organization as a whole.

Unfortunately, many of our conversations today are shallow, infrequent, rushed and increasingly of an electronic nature. In the workplace, most of us find ourselves overscheduled, double-booked and constantly running from meeting to meeting. When we do have a break, we tend to turn immediately to our BlackBerry, iPhone or other PDA of choice, to catch up on emails and voice mails.

This frenzied on-the-job atmosphere works against our ability to build and sustain one-on-one personal relationships. In fact, some of us have even started to see workplace conversations as a waste of time. How many times have you sent an email to someone who happens to be right down the hall? We're all guilty of it. More and more often, we favor taking action and producing results over building significant staff relationships through meaningful connections and conversations.

According to renowned author and speaker Margaret Wheatley, "There is no more powerful way to initiate significant change than to convene a conversation," (Wheatley, M., "Bringing Life to Organizational Change," *Journal of Strategic Performance Management*, 1998). However, many leaders and managers do not believe it's their job to promote and encourage conversations.

If you increase the meaning and the frequency of your conversations, you can boost employee engagement. According to a 2006 *Gallup Management Journal* study, only 29 percent of employees say they are strongly engaged in their work, and more than 70 percent say they are either not engaged or actively disengaged. However, Gallup researchers also found that leaders can interrupt employee disengagement by having meaningful conversations with these employees to strengthen their commitment.

Here are six specific strategies for promoting powerful conversations with colleagues, customers and everyone else in your life:

1. Create an environment of trust and mutual respect where all ideas are valued.

It is important to set and manage expectations about the types of behavior you deem appropriate within your organization. Your employees naturally look to you as a model of what is tolerated and what is not when it comes to interacting with others in the workplace. When you allow employees to be disrespectful and untrustworthy without consequence, you're sending a message that you accept these nonproductive behaviors. This also discourages others from speaking up and sharing their ideas. In this kind of negative environment, conversations tend to be more reserved, tentative and shallow. Give your team permission to hold everyone accountable for treating others with trust and respect. Once you create this type of environment, meaningful conversations will thrive.

2. Provide opportunities for all team members to share their unique perspectives.

Everyone has a unique perspective to share. However, some are more comfortable than others when it comes to contributing thoughts and ideas. We all know which one or two team members can be expected to "dominate" a conversation. Conversely, we often can predict which members of our team are least likely to jump in with their ideas. It's important to note that when some individuals choose not to speak up, it is not necessarily an indication that they have nothing to add. For some, it is simply more difficult to engage in public conversations given their communication style and preferences. That's why it's so important to reach out to everyone in the room to ensure that everyone has an opportunity to offer their opinion.

3. Build time into your schedule for meaningful conversations.

As a leader, you may feel like you're being pulled in a million different directions at any given moment. However, it's important to find the time to carry on meaningful conversations with your team. Commit a set amount of time each week to walking around the office or "rounding." Mark your calendar and stick to it.

4. Slow down and really listen to what people are saying.

It is nearly impossible to carry on a meaningful conversation with someone when you are not truly "present." Too often, our minds wander to other commitments or other conversations we need to have. As a result, we catch only a portion of what the person sitting directly across from us is saying. In many cases, instead of truly listening, you might be busy preparing your retort or next response. This unproductive practice is called "reloading." Reloading often results in an awkward moment or a blank stare from the other person because your statement bears no relevance to what she just said. If you tune into the other person instead of focusing on your next response, you'll find it much easier to maintain the natural back and forth flow of a meaningful conversation.

5. Manage your use of electronic devices.

In today's digital age, nearly everyone owns some sort of mobile device or personal digital assistant, whether it's a BlackBerry, iPhone, Droid or one of many tablets. How many times have you been in a meeting where participants are busy answering emails or surfing the web instead of listening? Out of respect for others, and in an effort to promote more meaningful conversations, you may want to enforce some PDA etiquette, requiring that PDAs are kept in their holsters during meetings and one-on-one conversations. While electronic devices have boosted productivity in many important ways, they also can create a barrier to quality conversations with others.

6. Anchor your conversations in values.

Discuss your organization's core values and ask your employees how they see those values in their own lives. How committed are they to those ideals? How do they demonstrate those values in their behaviors? But remember, a commitment to values, such as honesty, respect or teamwork, may not "look" the same to every individual. For example, if teamwork is a core value of your organization, ask your employees: "What does teamwork look like to you? What would we be doing if we had more teamwork in our department?"

By building masterful relationships one conversation at a time, you will build value for your employees, your customers and your entire organization. I invite you to create more space and time for meaningful conversations by following these six strategies.

CHAPTER

8

Round Regularly

Fit leaders take time to walk around the office and carry on informal conversations with their staff members. As I mentioned in Chapter 7, this practice is called "rounding."

We all spend time talking with our teams in formal meetings. But how can we as leaders become more visible and accessible to our people? By spending time in informal conversations with your team members and giving them an opportunity to share their concerns, ask questions or simply tell you about their current projects. Rounding allows you to do all this and more.

You can build powerful relationships with your team through these informal meetings and casual conversations. All you have to do is take time to stop by their offices and ask questions. Plus, you may just find out something you may have otherwise never learned.

Commit a set amount of time each week to "rounding" or walking around the office and talking to individual team members. You'll be surprised at what you discover.

If you want to become a successful "rounder," ask yourself these questions:

ROUNDING EXERCISE

- How much time do you currently spend just walking around the office?

- How much time will you devote to rounding in your organization?

- What types of information are more likely to emerge from a more casual encounter with staff?

- What times of the day, week and the month are the most suitable for you to make rounds?

- What would the value be to you if other members of your team were to round, as well?

See page 147 for exercise worksheet.

1) Set Clear Expectations 2) Remove Ambiguity 3) Take Time for Reflection 4) Know What Keeps Your Customers Up at Night
5) Stay Focused 6) Ask Open-Ended Questions 7) Make Time for Meaningful Conversations **8) Round Regularly**
9) Articulate Your Mission, Vision and Values 10) Sort and Prioritize Opportunities Competing for Your Attention

The Valuable (and Sometimes Surprising) Benefits of Rounding

At one point in my career, I managed people in 10 different offices around the country. I realized that if I wanted to help these employees feel connected to what we were doing in our headquarters office, I needed to make myself more visible and visit each office on a regular basis. This gave me an opportunity to learn first-hand what people were working on, and also it provided me with an opportunity to share my priorities and influence what was going on in other parts of the company.

So, every quarter I made a point to visit three or four of our regional offices. I'd spend an entire day in each regional office, and I would essentially conduct an account review. Everyone in the office was invited to attend this all-day meeting where we reviewed our relationships with all of our clients. It gave everyone in the office a chance to talk a little bit about what they were working on, and it gave me an opportunity to ask questions and to share my observations.

While I was visiting each regional office, I always spent the first half hour or so rounding. I'd walk around the office, say hello to people and introduce myself if there was a new employee.

Before I visited the San Francisco office one year, I had just approved a new position. One of my directors had asked if she could hire another staff person, and I asked her to present me with a business case. So, she put together a written case and I reviewed it. I told her to go ahead and hire another person, and she did. I happened to be visiting the San Francisco office about two or three weeks after the new employee came on board, and while I was rounding I had a chance to meet her.

"Welcome!" I said as I walked into her office. "It's nice to have you on board."

"Thank you!" she responded with a smile.

"So," I asked, "what are you working on?"

She looked at me and answered, "Well, actually not much of anything."

Obviously, I was a little taken aback. "My boss and I haven't really had a chance to sit down and go over what she wants me to work on," she explained.

Of course, the next stop I made was my director's office. "I just met your new employee, and she's really sharp," I said. "And I happened to ask her about what she's working on and she said not much of anything. You know, I read your business case for adding a new position and I agreed with you and approved the new hire—and it seems like she's just been sitting around for the last two to three weeks."

The director explained that she'd been so busy she hadn't had time to sit down with the new employee, and we had a long discussion about it. But the point is that I never would have learned about this if I hadn't been rounding.

There are certain things you can never learn unless you're just out and about and informally engaging in these conversations. What I discovered during my rounds that day allowed me to help my staff focus and get their priorities straight. It gave me a chance to explain that we've got to make the time to orient and train our people. Otherwise, it defeats the purpose of bringing them on board.

This is exactly why it's so important to get out and round.

1) Set Clear Expectations 2) Remove Ambiguity 3) Take Time for Reflection 4) Know What Keeps Your Customers Up at Night
5) Stay Focused 6) Ask Open-Ended Questions 7) Make Time for Meaningful Conversations 8) Round Regularly
9) Articulate Your Mission, Vision and Values 10) Sort and Prioritize Opportunities Competing for Your Attention

CHAPTER

9

Articulate Your Mission, Vision and Values

Fit leaders set direction for their organizations by clearly defining and articulating their mission, vision and values (MVV). This process allows leaders to establish a solid decision making platform and ensure their organizations move forward with a clear purpose and a basis for action.

Armed with a powerful mission and vision statement and a strong set of values, you and your team can make the smartest, most effective decisions for your organization. If you continually reinforce your mission, vision and values and ensure that all of your efforts are aligned around these statements, you will boost your team's performance and build resiliency at all levels of your organization.

A well-defined mission, vision and values set are crucial to the success of any business. It allows you and your team to stay on track as you work towards your organization's long-term goals. I explain how to define your MVV equation on the following page.

If you want to create a strong and clear basis for action, ask yourself the following questions:

MISSION, VISION AND VALUES EXERCISE

- What is the core purpose of your organization?

- How would you describe your team's contribution to the overall mission of the organization?

- What is the "why" of your organization that inspires others to go there with you?

- What organizational or team values drive the culture of your workforce?

- What is the gap between the values you currently see in your organization and the values you desire to see?

See page 148 for exercise worksheet.

Defining Your MVV Equation

As I mentioned at the beginning of this chapter, leaders set direction by clearly articulating the mission, vision and values of their organizations. Your organization will gain incredible power from a well-crafted mission and vision statement, which can be further amplified by a strong set of values.

Here is a step-by-step guide for defining your organization's mission, vision and values:

Step 1: Define Your Organization's Mission

MISSION = "What" work you are doing

Mission statements speak to what products, programs and/or services the organization or team delivers. A mission statement also tells us for whom this work is done.

Here are a couple of real world mission statements:

Pfizer Pharmaceutical's Mission Statement: *"We dedicate ourselves to humanity's quest for longer, healthier, happier lives through innovation in pharmaceutical, consumer and animal health products."*

Honest Tea's Mission Statement: *"Honest Tea seeks to create and promote great-tasting, healthy, organic beverages. We strive to grow our business with the same honesty and integrity we use to craft our recipes, with sustainability and great taste for all."*

EXERCISE: WHAT IS YOUR TEAM'S MISSION?

_____

_____

_____

Step 2: Define Your Organization's Vision

VISION = "Why" you are doing this work

Vision statements are short, succinct and inspiring. They speak to what your organization wants to become at some point in the future, often stretching your company's capabilities and self-image. An effective vision statement helps employees feel proud, excited and like they are part of something much bigger than themselves.

Here are a couple of real world vision statements:

Westin Hotels' Vision Statement: *"Year after year, Westin and its people will be regarded as the best and most sought after hotel and resort management group in North America."*

Amazon.com's Vision Statement: *"Our vision is to be earth's most customer centric company; to build a place where people can come to find and discover anything they might want to buy online."*

EXERCISE: WHAT IS YOUR TEAM'S VISION?

_____

_____

_____

_____

Together, a well-crafted mission and vision statement becomes the glue that binds the various parts of your organization together. These two statements also drive employee behavior.

Step 3: Define Your Organization's Values
VALUES = "How" people work

Values are the anchors we use to make decisions and consciously create the future we want. It's important to remember that your organization's values are not constrained by the past—you can adapt them to fit new situations.

Jim Kouzes and Barry Posner, researchers, authors and founders of The Leadership Challenge®, have found that shared values within an organization foster strong feelings of personal effectiveness, promote high levels of company loyalty, facilitate consensus around key organizational goals, promote strong norms about working and caring and reduce levels of job stress and tension.

Richard Barrett, founder of Barrett Values Centre and internationally known leadership consultant, has shown that when organizations unite around a shared set of values, they become more flexible, less hierarchical and less bureaucratic. When employees share not only the same values, but also the same mission and vision, organizational performance is significantly enhanced.

As a leader, your values define the organizational culture—and thus your organization's competitive advantage—when it comes to attracting and retaining talented people, building and sustaining high performance and building resiliency and adaptive capacity.

EXERCISE: WHAT ARE THE SHARED VALUES WITHIN YOUR ORGANIZATION?

1) Set Clear Expectations 2) Remove Ambiguity   3) Take Time for Reflection 4) Know What Keeps Your Customers Up at Night
5) Stay Focused   6) Ask Open-Ended Questions   7) Make Time for Meaningful Conversations 8) Round Regularly
9) Articulate Your Mission, Vision and Values   **10) Sort and Prioritize Opportunities Competing for Your Attention**

CHAPTER
10

Sort and Prioritize Opportunities Competing for Your Attention

Many leaders find it incredibly challenging to sort through and prioritize the often bewildering array of opportunities that compete for their attention. However, you simply cannot chase after every single opportunity that arises. If you view each opportunity as one worth pursuing, you'll create a stream of continuous demands that your team cannot possibly meet. In other words, if you fail to prioritize competing opportunities, you're setting up your team for failure.

As you work to formulate and fine-tune your strategy, take time to sift through, hand-pick and prioritize the most valuable opportunities. Once you create a priority list of opportunities, you'll have a clearer understanding of where to focus your organization's efforts and limited resources.

Are you properly prioritizing opportunities? Ask yourself these questions:

PRIORITIZING OPPORTUNITIES EXERCISE

- What are the key opportunities your organization could decide to pursue over the course of the next 12 months?

- What key opportunities are "in the bullseye" for your organization based upon market need and organizational strategy?

- What key opportunities would you pursue only on an opportunistic basis?

- How do you avoid becoming distracted by opportunities that simply remove your focus from what's most important?

- How do you communicate your priorities on a regular basis to focus your team's efforts?

See page 149 for exercise worksheet.

IN THE REAL WORLD

Targeting the Right Opportunities

Although you may be tempted to pursue every opportunity that arises, remember that not all opportunities are created equal. It's simply not realistic to run after every single opportunity that comes knocking. That's why it's important to sort through the array of opportunities, select the ones that most closely align with your key strategies and create a clear priority list.

I've noticed that most opportunities fall into one of four levels of focus. These four levels come together to create what I call an "Opportunity Board." Here is how it breaks down:

Level #1: Bullseye

These opportunities align with one or more of your organization's key strategies. When executed properly, these opportunities allow you to profitably serve your target markets—or they result in projects that yield exceptional benefits for your customers.

Level #2: In the Ballpark

These opportunities are close enough to your organization's "bullseye" to warrant your attention and evaluation. While they may not necessarily fall in your "sweet spot," these opportunities deserve your serious consideration once you've resourced opportunities in the "bullseye" area.

Level #3: Opportunistic Focus

These opportunities also are important and yet cannot be started right away as there may be a need for additional funding, authority or staffing. Once these constraints are lifted, these opportunities may be moved to the Bullseye or In the Ballpark sections of the Board.

Level #4: Off the Board

These opportunities are simply distractions that are capable of consuming precious resources that serve neither your strategies nor your customers. Do not pursue these opportunities unless you can make a strong case to senior management for doing so.

1) Set Clear Expectations 2) Remove Ambiguity   3) Take Time for Reflection 4) Know What Keeps Your Customers Up at Night
5) Stay Focused   6) Ask Open-Ended Questions   7) Make Time for Meaningful Conversations   8) Round Regularly
9) Articulate Your Mission, Vision and Values   10) Sort and Prioritize Opportunities Competing for Your Attention

Take Inventory

If you want to create an Opportunity Board, first take inventory and iden-tify the opportunities that your organization might pursue. Make a list of the key opportunities your organization could decide to pursue over the course of the next 12 months. Describe each of these opportunities in terms of the target mar-ket to be served, the customer need that would be met and the specific product or solution that would be delivered.

Once you have identified all viable opportunities, you can sort through and prioritize them, and move to a clearer understanding of where to focus your organization's efforts and limited resources.

My Opportunity Inventory

Build an Opportunity Board

Now, take each opportunity you identified in the Opportunity Inventory above and place them into one of the four levels of focus represented by different circles in the Opportunity Board.

Consider comparing your Opportunity Board with those of your peers to determine potential differences of opinion with regard to prioritizing major opportunities across the organization.

Place your completed Opportunity Board in the office where everyone can see it. By reviewing this board with your team, you'll increase your chances of pursuing and executing the "bullseye" opportunities that will lead to the most profitable results for your organization.

The Opportunity Board

Take the opportunities identified on the previous page
and place them into one of the four levels of focus.

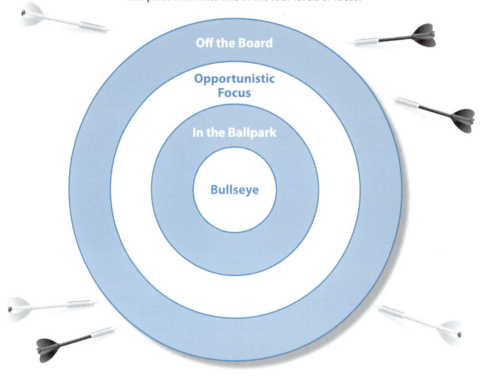

You have now created your Opportunity Board. Place this in the office where everyone can see it. When this happens, the probability increases substantially that great opportunities — those that are in your bullseye — will be pursued and executed.

PART 2

CONF**I**DENCE

The Second Face of Leadership Fitness

CONFIDENCE

An Introduction

In Part 1, I explained that fit leaders possess clarity, or a strong sense of direction. However, I have found that the most successful leaders combine this dynamic quality with a powerful self-confidence, which amplifies their message and allows them to intensify the clarity they bring to their team.

Over the course of my career, I have seen many incredibly intelligent leaders fail to succeed. More often than not, their failure came down to a lack of confidence. Even if a leader has ingenious plans and smart strategies, she cannot move forward if she has no confidence in her own ideas. If a leader does not fully appreciate her role in rallying the team around a new strategy or new direction, she will never prevail.

Fit leaders reach deep into their souls to muster the self-confidence they need to win. Whether you are trying to win senior management's buy-in or your team's commitment, it's important to remain confident. Employees have a keen sense, a sort of radar, when it comes to interpreting what they hear from their leaders. Your words may sound logical, but if you hesitate or if your message does not feel authentic, your team will quickly pick up on your insincerity. Once your employees sense that you do not really believe what you are espousing, your message has been compromised.

If you allow your uncertainties to go unresolved, you risk contaminating your messages with the self-doubting shadow that lurks behind your words. As I mentioned in the Introduction to this book, many leaders call these nagging doubts "gremlins" or "saboteurs." Regardless of how we label them, these doubts limit the power of our beliefs and intentions and get in the way of our overall impact.

Fit leaders have learned how to overcome the dampening effect of these potent, negative influences. They have developed "gremlin-fighting" strategies that allow them to push ahead with conviction and self-assurance.

Fit leaders also tend to be bold and optimistic. They are more likely to see the glass as half-full. However, while great leaders are certainly positive, they are not Pollyanna-ish. They do not have their heads in the clouds, nor do

11) Manage Your Inner Voices 12) Set Powerfully Bold Intentions 13) Convince Others to Follow Your Lead 14) Be Curious, Not Furious 15) Empower Others 16) Catch People Doing Things Right 17) Trust Others to Do Their Jobs 18) Reward Your People 19) Embrace Failure as an Essential Step in the Learning Process 20) Rely on a Repertoire of Positive Habits to Feed Your Confidence

they mislead themselves and their teams with blind optimism. Fit leaders have the clarity to know where the organization must head next, and they have the resilience and confidence necessary to bring others along with them.

One of the interesting things about confidence is that it is self-perpetuating. When you accomplish something important and significant because of your clarity and confidence, you actually become more confident. It's a lot like training for a race—the more you train, the more stamina you build and the stronger your body becomes. In the same way, when you push yourself beyond your normal leadership limits, you strengthen your confidence muscles and come back with more energy the next time around.

When you combine clarity with confidence, it leads to powerful results. If you want to be a confident leader, spend some time answering these questions:

- How can I quiet my inner "gremlins" and overcome self-doubt?

- How high am I setting the bar for my team?

- What can I do to convince others to follow my lead?

- How can I build my team's confidence by choosing to be curious, not furious?

- How can I empower team members and inspire them to stand behind my ideas?

- What steps can I take to catch my employees doing things right and acknowledge their accomplishments?

- How can I trust my employees to do their jobs?

- How can I reward my people and still preserve their intrinsic motivation?

- What can I do to embrace failure as an essential step in the learning process?

- What positive habits can I develop to feed my confidence?

In Chapters 11 through 20, I will walk through each of these questions to help you build confidence, the second face of leadership fitness.

CHAPTER
11

Manage Your "Inner Voices"

Even if you have a clear sense of direction and know exactly where you want to lead your team, self-doubt can block your path to success. If you allow those nagging, negative inner voices to consume you, you'll never gain the confidence you need to take action, move forward and achieve your goals.

As a leader, it's important to acknowledge that criticisms—both external and internal—will always be present. There's no getting around it. In fact, I have noticed that the bolder my vision and the bigger my plans, the louder my critical inner voices become. I have come to view the presence of these "gremlins" as confirmation that I am not playing small.

Fit leaders have the ability to lower the volume of negative inner voices so they can remain focused on the future.

If you want to better manage these derisive inner voices, ask yourself the following questions:

GREMLINS EXERCISE

- What negative inner voices are you hearing?

- What strategies do you use to manage self-doubt?

- What thoughts and behaviors feed your confidence despite the critical noise all around you?

- What's the worst thing that has happened to you when you moved forward with an idea or program you felt strongly about, despite the presence of nagging doubts?

- When have you been swayed by others to stop pursuing something you knew was right?

See page 152 for exercise worksheet.

IN THE REAL WORLD

Constructing Your Own Confidence Net™

Even when leaders become clear about where they want to take their teams, self-doubt can stop them dead in their tracks. All leaders are subject to resisters and critics, both external and internal. But with a little bit of practice, you can learn to overcome these negative voices.

In *Jump and the Net Will Appear* (New World Library, 2002), author Robin Crow claims that the obstacles holding us back are almost always internal. As a leader, your challenge is to manage these self-sabotaging "inner voices" so they do not block your forward movement.

As leaders chart new courses, they encounter many self doubts, including:
"You won't succeed."
"You'll fall on your face."
"You'll look like a fool."
"Who do you think you are?"

You can manage these doubts by being more aware of negative self-talk and recognizing that these unconstructive voices are distinct from your true intent. If you allow them to continue unchecked, these internal conversations will earn more credibility than they deserve.

In *Confidence: How Winning Streaks & Losing Streaks Begin & End* (Crown Business, 2004), author Rosabeth Moss Kanter points out that "everything can look like a failure in the middle." This can lead you to give up prematurely, just as you begin to "round the corner" and achieve your goals.

One strategy for inoculating yourself against the impact of powerful inner voices is to construct a personal safety net. Many people view safety nets as insurance to help them through life's unexpected shocks and stresses, such as a serious illness or job loss. However, leaders can also build a net to mitigate the effect and lower the volume of the various "inner voices" they'll invariably confront along the way to achieving greatness. I call this personal structure The Confidence Net™.

If you want to build a confidence net, develop a repertoire of positive habits that will feed your confidence and allow you to remain focused on your future—despite the noise all around you. In Chapter 20, I will ask you to think about the positive habits that increase your confidence and encourage you to incorporate one or more of these habits into your daily routine.

CHAPTER
12

Set Powerfully Bold Intentions

Fit leaders feed their employees' confidence by setting powerfully bold intentions for their teams. When leaders set the bar high, they demonstrate that they believe in their people.

When you tap into the power of intention, you and your team can reach seemingly unreachable goals. Dr. Wayne Dyer, an internationally renowned author and speaker in the field of self-improvement, believes that intention is much greater than just "determined ego or individual will."

"Intention is a field of energy that flows invisibly beyond the reach of our normal, everyday habitual patterns," Dr. Dyer writes in *The Power of Intention* (Hay House Inc., 2004). "We have the means to attract this energy to us and experience life in an exciting new way."

If you want to set powerful intentions for your team, ask yourself the following questions:

POWERFUL INTENTIONS EXERCISE

- How high are you setting the bar for your people?

- What is holding you back from going after even more?

- Where might you be setting your sights too low?

- How do you leverage the power of intention?

- What is the boldest intention you've set in the last six months?

See page 153 for exercise worksheet.

Setting the Bar High

Every year at open enrollment time, most organizations provide rather uninspiring packages to describe the newest changes to their employee benefit plans. So one year, I asked my Director of Employee Benefits to come up with a creative, engaging way to communicate the benefit changes to our employees. I even suggested that he could create a video featuring a series of skits to bring the changes to life. Not only would our employees enjoy the video, they could take it home to show their families. After all, it's often a significant other or another family member who helps an employee decide which benefits plan to choose.

Of course, as is the case in most corporate environments, we didn't have a lot of time to explore new, creative options. We were really down to the wire. However, I put out the challenge to my director to find a way to pull off this video in a limited amount of time.

Right off the bat, my director said, "David, there's no way we can do this. This is complex, and it's going to take a lot of time. We really need to think this through." I listened to my director and let him share what were pretty legitimate concerns. Yet, I again restated my intention of trying to make this happen, and I encouraged him to see past all the reasons that it wasn't possible.

The next day, my director came back into my office, and said, "David, I figured it out. I found a vendor that has a studio a few miles from our office. All we need to do is develop a script, and they will tape us and produce the videos in enough time to distribute them to our people."

I could tell that he was very proud. He had made it happen, and he felt great about it.

When you challenge an employee to do something he doesn't believe is possible, and then he actually accomplishes it, you help him break through his own self-imposed limitations. Too often, employees make up limitations such as "Oh, we don't have enough time," or "We don't have enough resources. There's no way we can do this." Sometimes, it takes a leader to encourage and challenge employees to focus on how it *can* be done rather than how it *can't* be done.

As a leader, your role is to set the bar high and enable your people to accomplish things well beyond what they think is possible. Once you do that, your people will be forever thankful to you. There is nothing more powerful than setting an intention and helping someone see they can actually achieve far more than they believe. This instills confidence in your employees and sets them up for continued success.

Of course, you don't want to set the bar so high that people fall and hurt themselves. Often, though, leaders can see the possibility, and sometimes it just takes a little pushing and confidence to help an employee see that possibility, as well. More often than not, if you show your people that you have confidence in them to pull something off, that's all the motivation they need to accomplish it on their own.

I showed my director that I was confident he could make this video happen even though he didn't think he could. I communicated my confidence to him, and he made it happen—and, he felt great about his accomplishment. As leaders, that's exactly what we want: to help our people and our organization achieve greatness. We can do just that by setting the bar high.

11) Manage Your Inner Voices 12) Set Powerfully Bold Intentions **13) Convince Others to Follow Your Lead** 14) Be Curious, Not Furious 15) Empower Others 16) Catch People Doing Things Right 17) Trust Others to Do Their Jobs 18) Reward Your People 19) Embrace Failure as an Essential Step in the Learning Process 20) Rely on a Repertoire of Positive Habits to Feed Your Confidence

CHAPTER
13

Convince Others to Follow Your Lead

Fit leaders have the ability to "sell" their ideas to their boss, their colleagues and their customers. Former Chrysler Chairman Lee Iacocca once noted, "You can have brilliant ideas, but if you can't get them across, your ideas won't get you anywhere." That's why the most accomplished leaders know how to effectively communicate their ideas and convince others to follow their lead.

If you want to "close the deal," it's important to do your homework, listen, adjust for your audience's communication preferences, present with passion and follow up "after the sale." Above all else, realize that when you receive an objection, this is often a signal your audience is interested in continuing the conversation—but you may need to provide them with more information to overcome their initial resistance. After all, an objection rarely means "No."

If you want to "sell" your ideas and convince others to follow your lead, ask yourself the following questions:

CONVINCING OTHERS TO FOLLOW EXERCISE

- What contributes to your success when it comes to winning people over?

- How often do you bury your audience in piles of numbers and analyses and lose the opportunity to connect your ideas to real results?

- How often do you interpret an objection as a "no" rather than as a signal that your audience simply needs more information?

- How consistently do you adapt your presentation to your audience's unique communication preferences?

- How effectively do you follow up "after the sale?

See page 154 for exercise worksheet.

Selling Your Ideas

Even if you are convinced you have an ingenious idea, it probably won't be implemented unless you can convince *others* that it is an ingenious idea. That's why it's important to learn how to effectively "sell" your ideas to your boss, your colleagues and your customers. With strong leadership, communication and planning, you can gain support and convince others to follow your lead.

In *The Art of Woo: Using Strategic Persuasion to Sell Your Ideas* (Penguin Group, 2007), G. Richard Shell and Mario Moussa write about how leaders can sell their ideas without coercion, using "relationship-based, emotionally intelligent persuasion."

If you want to win others over and effectively close the deal, consider following these ten practices:

1. Sell the Solution

If you want to gain support for your idea, sell the *solution* to your audience. Too often, leaders miss the point and confuse their audience with too many trivial details. They fail to stay focused on the final outcome or desired solution. When you inundate your boss and other key stakeholders with piles of numbers and analyses, you lose the opportunity to connect your ideas to real results they can see.

2. Answer the S.W.I.F.T. Question

If you are too focused on your own needs or how a new idea will make your life easier, you probably will not convince others to follow your lead. Instead, focus on how your ideas line up with the company's agenda and your boss' needs.

Before you try to sell an idea, ask yourself the S.W.I.F.T. question: "So, What's In It For Them?" The bottom line is your audience is often more interested in implementing their *own* ideas and plans. When you can answer the S.W.I.F.T. question, you'll increase your chances of securing the support you need from others.

3.   Appreciate Objections

Don't interpret every objection as a "no." Often, an objection is a signal that your audience wants to continue the conversation, and it may simply be a request for more information. With a little time, many people will actually overcome their own objections if you resist the temptation to pack your bags and declare the game over.

4.   Do Your Homework

A lack of preparation will doom your presentation before you even utter the first word. Take time to connect your ideas and recommendations to your organization's existing strategy and priorities. Try to anticipate questions and prepare appropriate responses. Do some research so you can provide sufficient background, rationale, timelines and financial impact. When you do your homework, you'll make a more credible case.

You may also want to run your ideas by trusted colleagues before you make the pitch to your boss. A colleague can provide you with important feedback, help you practice your approach and build your confidence.

5.   Listen—Don't Reload

When you are presenting an idea, it is critical to remain open to others' perspectives. If you are extremely passionate about your position, your audience may misinterpret your level of clarity and energy and assume that you are closed-minded and resistant to other ideas. How can you prevent this from happening? By listening to others.

Unfortunately, many leaders practice a technique referred to as "reloading". When you reload, you are formulating your next statement while the other person is speaking. Reloading limits the effectiveness of your communication because you are too busy preparing your response to pay attention to the other person. Consequently, you miss important cues that can help you properly address others' objections or questions. When you reload, your audience will quickly catch on to the fact that you are not really listening.

6.   Adjust for Communication Preferences

If you understand your colleagues' unique communication preferences, you'll know how to effectively address them, respond to their questions and gain their support for your ideas. Many organizational leaders have completed some inventory of their personality or communication styles (e.g., DiSC, Myers Briggs, etc.). If you use this crucial information as you prepare your pitch, you'll know how to approach each individual in the most effective way.

7. Start with the End

A whopping 60 percent of people are global processors—they look at the big picture first and then assimilate the facts that created the big picture. Another 30 percent of people are analytic processors. These people start with "facts" and then assemble the big picture after analysis. Only 10 percent of people combine both processes.

Therefore, it's wise to open your pitch with the big picture or the recommendation you want people to walk away with. By doing so, you'll grab the attention of 70 percent of most audiences.

8. Present with Passion

When it comes time to pitch your idea, bring every iota of energy and enthusiasm you have to your presentation. Use visual aids when appropriate, maintain eye contact with your audience and avoid annoying, nervous movements.

9. Tell Them Three Times

Take advantage of one of the most time-tested strategies for successful public speaking: First, tell your audience what you are going to tell them. Secondly, go ahead and tell them. Lastly, tell them what you told them. This surprisingly simple yet effective technique employs the power of repetition to reinforce your main messages.

10. Follow Up After the "Sale"

After all your hard work preparing and delivering your pitch, you have secured support for your ideas. You have effectively closed the deal. Or have you?

If you win initial support from your boss or others in your organization, this is cause for celebration—not complacency. Never underestimate the importance of follow-through. When you follow up with your audience and continually reinforce the value of the ideas you just sold, you'll help them avoid "buyers' remorse"—and you'll maintain their ongoing support.

CHAPTER
14

Be Curious, Not Furious

Fit leaders do not jump at the opportunity to tell colleagues why they are wrong or point out how their logic is faulty. When team members (particularly leaders) constantly disagree and furiously shoot down everyone else's perspective, the flow of ideas will abruptly come to an end. In this environment, employees or colleagues will quickly lose confidence and learn to keep their mouths shut.

On the other hand, when you choose to be curious instead of furious, you invite others to willingly share their ideas and keep their contributions at a high level. If a team member presents an idea you do not agree with, don't reject it. Instead, ask him a few open-ended questions. This not only invites your colleague to consider the consequences or implications of his thinking—it also builds his confidence and serves as a learning experience for your entire team.

Are you a curious leader or a furious leader? Ask yourself these questions:

CURIOSITY EXERCISE

- How do you demonstrate your genuine curiosity and interest in others' thoughts and ideas?

- What is your public response when members of your team shoot down others' ideas before attempting to understand them?

- What impact will you have on your team if you choose to be *furious* (disagree first, ask questions later) instead of *curious*?

- How can curiosity advance and encourage your team's learning process?

- What is the benefit of being curious even when you know the answers to your questions?

See page 155 for exercise worksheet.

Choose to Be Curious—or Get Soaked!

At one point in my career, I led a team of about ten people. Two of these people were consistently negative about any new ideas their colleagues suggested. It was really getting in our way, and it was destroying the team's spirit of openness. The other team members got really discouraged. They would think they had something interesting to contribute, and then one or both of these individuals would always attack the idea.

So, I decided it was time to teach the team to be more curious about everyone's ideas. Now, I don't necessarily recommend that everyone try this at home—but I went out and bought some Nerf water pistols. At the beginning of our next meeting, I gave a water pistol to each team member and said, "I give each of you permission to unload on anyone who responds to an idea by being negative...anyone who starts by being furious instead of being genuinely curious about what it is that the other person is saying." Of course, the team members were delighted.

As you can imagine, two particular team members got pretty wet. It only took a couple of "Super Soaker" meetings for these two nay-saying individuals to get the point. They quickly learned that I was trying to create an environment where anyone could say anything and trust that the team would seek to understand their ideas.

In some cases, after the team had an opportunity to ask questions, they decided not to adopt the new idea. Yet, from that day forward, we never did anything to close down a team member's willingness to contribute, or meet ideas with a furious response instead of a curious one.

Put an end to furious responses

As I watch my clients interact in team meetings, I often see people jump too quickly to beat down a colleague's idea. This is what I call a furious response. When you choose to disagree first and ask questions later, your colleague often feels attacked. More often than not, she'll get defensive and dig in her heels more deeply in support of her original position.

When you are trying to help a colleague see a different point of view, the last thing you want her to do is become defensive. If you are genuinely interested in engaging her in a discussion around alternatives, you want her to remain open to the possibility that she may not have the only viable idea or solution.

Choose to be *curious*, not furious. If you disagree with a team member's idea, even if you believe she is wrong, begin by asking her an open-ended question.

Most good open-ended questions begin with a "What" or a "How," and they cannot be answered with a simple "Yes" or "No." For example, you might ask, "What impact will your suggested solution have on the underinsured population?" or "How do you see this new policy working on the weekends?"

When you look closely at these two questions, you can see that I am concerned with how the proposed solution might play out in certain circumstances. Rather than just coming out and saying why I think the solution is impractical, I come at it from a place of curiosity. I invite my colleague to think more deeply with me about the consequences or implications of her thinking.

When you follow this approach, you'll accomplish several outcomes. First and foremost, your employee or colleague will not have the common defensive reaction that usually accompanies pushback from a leader. Instead, you will encourage a dialogue that is motivated by your interest in learning more about your colleague's approach or thinking.

Secondly, when you take this curious approach, you'll advance your team's education. By asking clarifying questions, you'll encourage everyone to take the proposed solution to a deeper level, test it and make sure it holds up under pressure. Oftentimes, the most robust, practical solutions are the ones created by multiple team members.

Thirdly, your employees and colleagues will appreciate that you place value and importance on their ideas. If everyone is busy advocating for their own point of view by weakening everyone else's contributions, the team will never develop the best solutions. When team members choose to be curious, they invite others to share their ideas willingly.

As you take a more curious approach, remember to validate your employees' ideas. Let's say you have just presented a new idea to me. How would it make you feel if I started out by saying, "That's a really interesting approach. I haven't thought of it in exactly that way. I'm curious to hear how you think this approach could impact the uninsured?" Chances are you would feel good that you've come up with an interesting approach. You would feel like you have been heard and understood. And you would feel engaged and willing to answer my question about the impact of your idea. In the course of our ensuing conversation, you might even modify your approach based on our discussion.

This is a much more respectful way to engage in conversation with your colleagues. When your team takes a curious approach, not only will your meetings become more civil, but you'll also create an environment where everyone looks forward to a healthy exchange of various perspectives.

CHAPTER
15

Empower Others

Fit leaders cultivate followers by empowering others with inspirational ideas. In other words, confident leaders know how to win over the hearts and minds of their people.

If you want to develop a true followership, you cannot simply provide direction and expect people to get on board. It's also important to embolden your team members, feed their confidence, ignite their passions and inspire them to stand behind your ideas. Once you accomplish this feat, people will follow wherever you may lead.

Do you empower others and inspire them to follow you? Ask yourself the following questions:

EMPOWERMENT EXERCISE

- How do you ignite a spark that compels others to get behind your ideas?

- What gets in the way of your people getting on board with your program?

- How do your energize your team?

- What does empowerment look and feel like to you?

- What empowers you?

See page 156 for exercise worksheet.

11) Manage Your Inner Voices 12) Set Powerfully Bold Intentions 13) Convince Others to Follow Your Lead 14) Be Curious, Not Furious **15) Empower Others** 16) Catch People Doing Things Right 17) Trust Others to Do Their Jobs 18) Reward Your People 19) Embrace Failure as an Essential Step in the Learning Process 20) Rely on a Repertoire of Positive Habits to Feed Your Confidence

Igniting Employees with a Core Purpose

One way you can inspire and motivate your team members to follow you is by creating a core philosophy. This "central idea" or "core purpose" gives your people a sense of confidence and a reason to come to work every day.

Typically, your organization's core purpose is simply the company's "reason for being." It's rarely about making money, and it is often distinct from your organization's specific goals and business strategies.

For example, Coca Cola's core purpose is to "refresh the world." Therefore, if you are a Coca Cola employee, everything you do and every choice you make needs to support this philosophy. So, as each employee develops, produces, promotes or delivers a Coca Cola product, they need to satisfy this overall purpose of refreshing the world.

Here are a few other real world examples of core purposes for well-known companies:

COMPANY	CORE PURPOSE
3 M	To solve unsolved problems innovatively
WALT DISNEY	To make people happy
MARY KAY	To give unlimited opportunity to women
MARRIOTT	To make people away from home feel they are among friends and really wanted
NIKE	To experience the emotion of competition, winning and crushing competitors

As you work to define or communicate your organization's core purpose, answer the following question with your team members:

What is my core motivation?
I go to work each day because I want to: _____

_____

Once your people understand their core motivation, they will be inspired to move forward and make choices that support that purpose.

CHAPTER 16

Catch People Doing Things Right

A fit leader builds her team's confidence and encourages them to achieve greatness by recognizing each employee's accomplishments. Unfortunately, while most of us are adept at catching people doing things wrong, few of us make a point to catch people doing things right.

With a little attention, you can increase your awareness of the good all around you. Look for opportunities to pat your employees on the back and feed their confidence. When you provide sufficient praise to your team members, you will notice they are much more confident and receptive when it comes time for you to offer them constructive or corrective feedback.

If you want to catch your people doing the right thing, ask yourself the following questions:

POSITIVE FEEDBACK EXERCISE

- How often do you provide positive feedback to members of your team?

- What impact does your praise have on overall employee confidence and engagement?

- How do you keep track of the positive accomplishments of your people?

- What is your ratio of positive to constructive feedback?

- What other approaches do you take to build up the confidence of your staff?

See page 157 for exercise worksheet.

IN THE REAL WORLD

Filling Up Your Team's Emotional Bank Account

It's incredibly easy to catch people doing things wrong—and unfortunately, many leaders have a hard time catching people doing things right. After all, most of our performance review systems were designed to identify weaknesses and point out areas for improvement.

However, I've discovered that when we offer our employees sufficient praise for their behaviors, attitudes and successes, they are much more receptive when we do have to provide them with constructive or corrective feedback.

When discussing the benefits of positive feedback, author and leadership authority Stephen R. Covey often uses the metaphor of an "emotional bank account." Here's how it works: When you offer positive feedback to an employee, you are making a "deposit" into that individual's emotional bank account. So, when you regularly catch people doing things right and praise them for it, you're filling up their accounts. Then, when you do have to make a "withdrawal" by giving an employee constructive feedback, you won't leave him with a "deficit."

In other words, if you take every opportunity to provide positive feedback, your employees will always have a surplus in their emotional bank accounts. This will make things much easier when you need to make a "withdrawal" by pointing out a mistake or discussing something an employee needs to change or improve.

Social science researcher and positive psychology pioneer Dr. Barbara Fredrickson discusses a similar concept in her book *Positivity: Groundbreaking Research Reveals How to Embrace the Hidden Strength of Positive Emotions, Overcome Negativity, and Thrive* (Crown Archetype, 2009). During her research, Dr. Fredrickson found that people benefit from a positive to constructive feedback ratio of at least 3 to 1. Therefore, if you can give your employees positive praise three times for every one time you have to give them constructive criticism, they should be okay at the end of the day.

This is just more evidence that leaders need to stay focused on catching people doing things right. Try to be almost aggressive in calling employees out on their accomplishments and acknowledging their great work. Because when it comes down to it, that's what people want: They want to be acknowledged, they want to be noticed and they want to be seen. Far too often, we only give people that recognition when they do something wrong. It's time to catch people doing things right!

CHAPTER
17

Trust Others to Do Their Jobs

Fit leaders instill confidence in their employees by trusting team members to do their jobs. In other words, successful leaders do *not* micro-manage their people.

If you want to cultivate confidence in your employees, give them the opportunity to figure out how to accomplish their work. Do not constantly interfere or re-capture work that you have already delegated or assigned to others.

When you immediately jump in at the first sign of failure or misalignment, you short-circuit your employee's learning process. Plus, from that day forward, the employee will assume that you'll always step in and save the day when he does not know how to handle a project.

Are you a micro-manager or do you trust your employees to do their jobs? Ask yourself the following questions:

TRUST EXERCISE

- How often do you micromanage others?

- How do you instill confidence in your team members?

- How do you remind yourself to let others complete the projects you have assigned to them?

- How do you stay focused on the big picture?

- What successes have you had when you trusted others to do their jobs?

See page 158 for exercise worksheet.

11) Manage Your Inner Voices 12) Set Powerfully Bold Intentions 13) Convince Others to Follow Your Lead 14) Be Curious, Not Furious 15) Empower Others 16) Catch People Doing Things Right **17) Trust Others to Do Their Jobs** 18) Reward Your People 19) Embrace Failure as an Essential Step in the Learning Process 20) Rely on a Repertoire of Positive Habits to Feed Your Confidence

IN THE REAL WORLD

Don't Take the Monkey Off Their Backs

Over the course of my career, I have seen far too many leaders take back an assignment from an employee because he thought he could handle it better himself. This is a toxic, yet all too common, leadership mistake.

Once you delegate a task to a team member, do *not* take it back—even if the project is not going as smoothly as you had hoped. While you may be tempted to finish your employee's work because you think it will be easier or faster, remember that you would be doing a terrible disservice to your team member. Not only will you disempower her and tear down her confidence, but you will also set a terrible precedent: Your team members will assume that you'll always swoop in and save the day when a project is not going well.

Work-life expert and best-selling author Barbara Moses once said, "If you allow staff to own a project, you must trust in their capacity and avoid micro-management. Be there to provide support when needed, but don't force yourself into the picture."

So, when an employee comes into your office with a monkey on his back, don't take it off for him. Of course, you can offer some guidance and walk him through a few suggestions of how he may be able to complete the assignment. But when he leaves your office, that monkey should still be on his back. It's up to him to get rid of it.

If you allow the employee to solve the problem on his own, you will prove that you trust him to complete his work in a satisfactory manner. And when he *does* accomplish the task, he'll gain the confidence he needs to take on the next big challenge he encounters.

CHAPTER
18

Reward Your People

Fit leaders reward employees in ways that preserve their intrinsic motivation. Too often, leaders focus on short-term or "extrinsic" rewards, like cash, gifts or vacation days. Leaders who rely on these one-dimensional rewards diminish their employees' confidence and natural pride associated with doing a good job.

In *Drive: The Surprising Truth About What Motivates Us* (Riverhead, 2009), author Daniel H. Pink points out that an overreliance on carrots and sticks, or what we would call extrinsic motivators, can actually decrease employee productivity and engagement.

As a leader, focus on leveraging higher level rewards or "intrinsic" motivators. You can do this by creating an environment where your employees enjoy autonomy, have opportunities to achieve mastery and can commit to a common, lofty purpose. Together, these three factors will keep your people engaged, empowered and confident.

Do you reward your employees in ways that nurture their intrinsic motivation? Ask yourself the following questions:

REWARDING EXERCISE

- What personally motivates you to excel?

- How are you respecting your team members' need for autonomy?

- What is the "why" behind the goals and activities of your organization?

- In what areas of their work do your people have opportunities to achieve mastery?

- How long-lasting are the effects of some of the more traditional "carrot and stick" rewards you have used in the past?

See page 159 for exercise worksheet.

Why Money Isn't the Most Powerful Motivator

As leaders, we often struggle to retain our best people. Naturally, many of us turn to money to convince valuable employees to stay with our organizations. We think that as long as we pay our people well, they will be immune to the head hunters who are constantly calling and enticing them to consider other opportunities.

However, experienced leaders eventually discover that money is not the main motivator for our people. Money is only a short-term motivator or an "extrinsic" reward. Yes, we have to pay people fairly based on their responsibilities and the level of work they provide. Yet, once people are paid at a fair rate and they feel like their basic financial needs are being met, money quickly loses its motivational power. At this point, employees develop a higher level of professional needs.

For instance, employees want to feel like they're working on something important. People want to feel like their organization, and particularly their boss, cares about them and is looking out for their professional goals. They want to work on exciting, fulfilling projects. They need to have the freedom to create—and also the freedom to fail. Most professionals are looking for an environment where they are appreciated and have an opportunity to excel. These are all "intrinsic" rewards.

If you appreciate your people and provide them with opportunities to grow and move through the organization at an appropriate pace, they are much less likely to say yes to a recruiter—even if that recruiter is dangling more money in front of them. If an employee feels engaged in her work and supported by her organization and manager, she will probably tell that recruiter she isn't interested in other career opportunities.

On the other hand, if your employee does not feel valued, if she feels like she is not receiving these higher level rewards, she will probably accept a call from a recruiter. She may even take the next step and meet with a potential new employer.

In other words, when your people pursue other career opportunities, it's typically not because they are looking for more money. It's usually because some of these other "intrinsic" motivators are not present in their current job. Of course, any employee can leave an organization and make more money in the next job. However, when an employee decides to search for a new job, it's often not because he wants to make more money. It's often because he feels there is something else missing in his relationship with his employer.

As a leader, it's your job to recognize these signals. Have you created an environment where your employees can be autonomous, where they have opportunities to achieve mastery and can commit to a higher core purpose? If not, your people may not feel like their higher level needs are being met. If you want to instill confidence in your employees and keep them committed to the organization, address their needs for autonomy, mastery and the feeling that they're working towards some noble purpose.

11) Manage Your Inner Voices 12) Set Powerfully Bold Intentions 13) Convince Others to Follow Your Lead 14) Be Curious, Not Furious 15) Empower Others 16) Catch People Doing Things Right 17) Trust Others to Do Their Jobs 18) Reward Your People **19) Embrace Failure as an Essential Step in the Learning Process** 20) Rely on a Repertoire of Positive Habits to Feed Your Confidence

CHAPTER
19

Embrace Failure as an Essential Step in the Learning Process

Fit leaders embrace failure as a powerful learning experience. Leaders face many uncertainties as they make important decisions for their organizations. They may question whether or not to enter or abandon a new product line, whether customers will support a new pricing schedule or whether they should distribute products directly through an intermediary. Many leaders fear that if they take a risk, they will fail.

However, your job is not to *eliminate* risk from decision making. Your job is to *manage* risk. You can accomplish this by maintaining clarity and confidence as you weigh the pros and cons of each option.

Unfortunately, organizations sometimes create barriers to risk-taking—even when they claim to value innovation and experimentation. When an employee tries something new and fails, how do you respond? Do you embrace failure as an essential step in the learning process or do you punish the employee for not reaching the goal? If you want to be a fit leader, it's important to embrace failures—both your own and your employees'.

If you want to learn how to embrace failure, ask yourself these questions.

EMBRACING FAILURE EXERCISE

- What actions do you take to promote risk taking in your organization?

- What actions do you take that might discourage risk taking?

- What happens when someone in your organization takes a risk and fails?

- Where have you failed in the last twelve months?

- How is the fear of failure holding you back?

See page 160 for exercise worksheet.

Learning from Failure

According to legend, it took Thomas Edison 1,000 tries to invent the light bulb. In other words, he "failed" a whopping 999 times before he reached success. (Not surprising, considering that he was working on his invention in the dark!)

Soon after Edison revealed his earth-shattering invention, a French reporter asked, "Mr. Edison, how did it feel to fail 999 times?" As the story goes, Thomas Edison just smiled and replied, "Young man, I have not failed 999 times. I have simply found 999 ways how *not* to create a light bulb."

In other words, Thomas Edison learned from his mistakes—and he refused to be discouraged by those 999 botched experiments. Most mortals would have given up much sooner. Yet each failure taught Edison something important that allowed him to go back and tweak the process or switch out the components until he finally got it right.

I myself have failed many times in my career, but one particularly painful failure always stands out in my mind. It all started when a healthcare information company hired me to develop a brand new product line for two very big-name customers. At the very outset, my boss told me that the company knew this was a high-risk project. However, the project had the potential to lead to all kinds of opportunities—we could build a whole new part of our business around this product. Because I had experience in this particular area, they really wanted me to lead this development team.

So, I decided to come aboard and take on the challenge. I worked on the project and led the team for about two years. However, at the end of that arduous two-year period, I came to an alarming realization: we were not going to succeed. We just weren't going to pull it off. Even though we had made some progress and created some headway in this new area, in the end our customers were not supportive of what we had created.

I had to conclude that this two-year project was a failure. And this was something new to me. Up until that point, I had enjoyed one career success after another. So I was thinking, "Gee, maybe I should leave the company. I'll never be able to do anything else here. I'm a failure."

You see, when we fail, we tend to personalize it. That's exactly what I did. In my mind, it wasn't that the *project* failed—*I* failed. I spent about two months feeling really miserable. I was trying to figure out what to do, and I talked to my wife about it every night. Eventually, I realized that the company did not see me

11) Manage Your Inner Voices 12) Set Powerfully Bold Intentions 13) Convince Others to Follow Your Lead 14) Be Curious, Not Furious 15) Empower Others 16) Catch People Doing Things Right 17) Trust Others to Do Their Jobs 18) Reward Your People **19) Embrace Failure as an Essential Step in the Learning Process** 20) Rely on a Repertoire of Positive Habits to Feed Your Confidence

as a failure. As a matter of fact, they followed through on their original promise. They told me from the very beginning that this was a risky project, but they still wanted to give it a shot—and if it didn't turn out to be successful, it would be okay and we would learn from it. And that's exactly what happened.

In the end, instead of running away from the failure, I embraced it as an essential step in my learning process. I decided to stay with the company, and I went on to become the VP of Product Development, then the General Manager for the largest business unit and eventually the Executive VP of the entire organization. It was a great experience. And had I not embraced failure, had I run from it instead of learning from it, I never would have been as successful as I was at the company.

I think there are two lessons here: One is that leaders really need to stick to their promises. For example, when an organization says, "We view this as risky, and if it doesn't work out it's going to be okay," they really need to follow through with that. As a leader in your organization, you need to nurture an environment where an employee can fail without it having negative consequences on her career.

Secondly, any employee or individual who leads a failed project needs to embrace that failure as an essential step in the learning process. Success is not a linear journey—most leaders do not have careers that advance in a straight line. In reality, you go up, and you come down a little bit and then you go up again.

It may seem counterintuitive, but the people who have been the most successful in life and in business are the people who have failed the most. Therefore, your ability to fail is directly related to your long-term success.

CHAPTER
20

Rely on a Repertoire of Positive Habits to Feed Your Confidence

Fit leaders accumulate and consistently perform a repertoire of positive habits that help to feed their confidence. For countless decades, psychology experts have pointed out that anyone can develop a good habit if they practice the new behavior for about 21 days. Using this "21-day rule," you can cultivate positive habits that will boost your confidence as you navigate through uncharted territory.

Of course, every leader has a distinctive set of confidence-building habits. For some, it is simply the kind of clothes they wear. For others, it is daily exercise, a nutritious breakfast or meditation. Regardless of the unique routine you follow, it's important to continually rely on a repertoire of positive habits to build your confidence.

Are you nurturing your confidence with positive habits? Ask yourself the following questions:

POSITIVE HABITS EXERCISE

- What positive habits feed your confidence?

- What reminders or structures do you employ to maintain a positive focus?

- How long does it take you to establish a new pattern of behavior?

- What personal practices embolden you on a daily basis?

- What can you do to get out of your own way?

See page 161 for exercise worksheet.

IN THE REAL WORLD

The Mighty Power Suit

When I'm teaching in the Fit Leader's Program™ or Fit Leaders Academy, I often ask clients to identify behaviors or habits they practice on a regular basis that give them confidence. These are the habits that allow them to stay focused on their goals despite the noise and distractions surrounding them.

Many clients say that exercise is their primary confidence-building habit. They explain, "When I exercise, I feel like I'm in top form; I feel at the top of my game." Other people say it's prayer or meditation. They explain that praying or meditating calibrates their emotions and helps them begin their day feeling stronger. Still others point to a good night's sleep or, in my case, a power outfit.

In my workshop, I often use myself as an example of the positive effect a power outfit can provide. I explain that I have an outfit or two that always makes me feel very confident. So, if I have a very important meeting or if I'm giving a presentation, I will always wear this particular suit, shirt and tie. It got to the point where when my wife saw me wearing my power outfit, she would jokingly say, "Oh, I see you're wearing your uniform again." And I'd often answer, "Well you know, sweetie, I know it looks like I'm wearing the same outfit a lot, and when I wear it, it just makes me feel really good. It makes me feel almost invincible."

So, I often tell my class this story and encourage them to put together their own power outfit...and I always give them a caveat. I say, "You have to be careful to not wear the same outfit two days in a row, especially if you're going to see the same people."

One day I was wearing my power outfit in class and gave my students this warning. The very next day, I had a really important meeting, and I wore the same suit I'd worn the day before when I was teaching the class. Of course, I had on a different shirt, but it certainly looked the same because it was the same color.

Sure enough, I'm in the conference room waiting for the meeting to start, and as people started walking in, I saw someone I didn't expect to join the meeting—someone from my class. He had seen me in the "same" outfit the day before, when I had told his class to never wear the same outfit two days in a row. As he came into the room and saw me, he pointed his finger at me kind of like, "I gotcha!"

So, I was caught wearing the same outfit two days in row…not my greatest moment. But I still felt confident. Why? Because I was wearing my power outfit!

The moral of the story is that a positive habit or routine can go a long way to feeding your confidence. You just need to be careful…especially when it comes to wearing those power outfits a little too frequently.

PART 3

EFFECTIVENESS

[The Third Face of Leadership Fitness]

EFFECTIVENESS

An Introduction

Even if a leader possesses clarity and confidence, he will not excel unless he is also effective. A fit leader knows how to successfully implement and execute plans and achieve long-term results for his team and organization.

In my work with leaders, I have coached and trained many executives armed with large doses of clarity and confidence—and they lacked the effectiveness to accomplish anything. If you want to be a fit leader, it's essential to develop several key effectiveness skills: conflict resolution, delegation, feedback, succession management and leading change.

First and foremost, effective leaders know how to promote and resolve healthy conflict. Fit leaders can listen to objections and handle resistance without becoming defensive. They do not personalize issues, and they can call on several different conflict handling modes depending upon the situation. The best leaders realize that when they encourage healthy conflict within their team, they create powerful, meaningful discussions.

Fit leaders also excel at delegation—which is a struggle for many professionals. Often, leaders believe they can accomplish a task more quickly on their own or they simply don't think their employees can handle it. However, the most effective leaders are the ones who can trust their employees to accomplish important work. The organizational reach of a leader often grows in direct proportion to his ability to delegate.

Additionally, the most effective leaders know that feedback is one of the most powerful tools they can use to support and improve their team's performance. They realize if they provide feedback at the "teachable moment," or right after the triggering event or behavior, they will have the greatest impact on their employee's future performance.

Perhaps most importantly, effective leaders have the ability to facilitate successful transitions. They steer clear of complacency by creating a sense of urgency for their teams, and they help their people embrace change.

21) Establish Objectives that Focus on Results, Relationships and Renewal 22) Delegate Authority, Not Responsibility
23) Promote Healthy Conflict 24) Provide Feedback at the "Teachable Moment" 25) Realize That Past Performance Is No Guarantee
of Future Results 26) Hold Yourself Accountable 27) Defeat Complacency 28) Communicate Clearly and Often
29) Listen Actively 30) Develop Other Leaders

If you want to be a highly effective leader, ask yourself these questions:

- How can I set objectives that focus on results, relationships and renewal?

- What assignments and projects am I holding onto that others can do for me?

- What steps can I take to promote healthy conflict within my team?

- How well am I providing feedback at the "teachable moment"?

- How well do I accept that past accomplishments do not guarantee future success?

- How can I follow through on my promises and commitments and ensure my team does the same?

- What steps can I take to make sure my team's next transition is successful?

- How can I communicate more effectively with my employees?

- How often do I truly listen to my team members?

- How can I tap into my knowledge and experiences to develop other leaders?

In Chapters 21 through 30, I will walk through each of these questions and help you develop effectiveness, the third face of leadership fitness.

CHAPTER
21

Establish Objectives that Focus on Results, Relationships and Renewal

Fit leaders possess proficient interpersonal skills, and they establish employee objectives that develop this important trait in others.

When organizations only recognize and reward bottom-line results, leaders often get away with ignoring the important needs of employees and colleagues as long as they are meeting their financial objectives and organizational goals.

In the long run, you cannot sustain stellar results without the support and power granted by your employees. That's why it's important to look beyond final results and examine how your employees actually produce those results. In other words, measure the "how" along with the "what."

Consider developing objectives in three major categories: Results, Relationships and Renewal. I will describe these categories in detail in the Real World portion of this chapter.

Are you developing effective objectives for your team? Ask yourself the following questions:

ESTABLISHING OBJECTIVES EXERCISE

- What is the mix of Results, Relationship and Renewal objectives you have set for individuals on your team?

- What are some examples of Relationship objectives you might establish for members of your team?

- How many times throughout the year do you sit down to review progress against goals and objectives?

- What objectives have you set in the past year that stretched the capabilities of your team?

- How inspiring are the goals and objectives in your organization?

See page 164 for exercise worksheet.

21) Establish Objectives that Focus on Results, Relationships and Renewal 22) Delegate Authority, Not Responsibility
23) Promote Healthy Conflict 24) Provide Feedback at the "Teachable Moment" 25) Realize That Past Performance Is No Guarantee
of Future Results 26) Hold Yourself Accountable 27) Defeat Complacency 28) Communicate Clearly and Often
29) Listen Actively 30) Develop Other Leaders

IN THE REAL WORLD

The Three R's of Performance Management: Results, Relationships and Renewal

Many years ago, when I was a senior HR executive, my team and I decided to revamp our performance appraisal system. Like many other companies at the time, our organization's performance review and feedback process focused primarily on "end of year" discussions with each employee.

Most employees dreaded these annual sessions, and managers fretted over the hours they would spend completing the formal HR performance appraisal forms. To further complicate matters, many managers did not keep track of each employee's performance during the year. When it came time for them to fill out the annual forms, they were at a loss of what to say. Some did their best to recollect the past, while others just "made it up." Obviously, this was not the best system for assessing employee accomplishments and opportunities for improvement.

As we set out to design a better system, we agreed upfront that manager-employee performance discussions needed to occur more than once a year. We asked managers and employees to sit down at least three times a year to talk about performance, goals and professional development. This gave managers the opportunity to discuss and document each employee's performance while it was still fresh in their minds—as opposed to waiting until the end of the year and trying to recollect all the contributions the employee made in the past 12 months.

The new system also allowed managers to address performance issues throughout the year instead of ignoring problems until it was time to conduct a formal performance review. It also made it much easier for managers to complete their final annual review documents. All they had to do was look at their intermediate discussion forms and then write a summary. Managers were happy to discover the process was much more effective and far less time consuming.

In addition to increasing the number of performance discussions, we also developed a new framework for thinking about employee objectives. Rather than lumping all the objectives together, we asked managers and employees to think of objectives across three major categories: Results, Relationships and Renewal. We called these the **Three Rs**.

The first R (Results) is reserved for what we typically think about when we write objectives: the annual business outcomes we are seeking to accomplish.

Results objectives may include sales goals, process improvements, new product rollouts, etc. To be effective, these objectives must be specific and measurable. We need to know precisely what we are setting out to change and by how much. Results objectives should also be achievable and realistic. While we always want to include some element of "stretch" when setting employee objectives, we don't want to set our people up for failure if a target is not realistically within reach in the specified amount of time. Finally, we want to make sure objectives are time-bound so dates and deadlines are clear upfront.

The second R (Relationships) focuses on how employees treat others and how well they collaborate with their managers and other team members to achieve business results. I refer to this as interpersonal proficiency. When employees achieve short-term results by misbehaving or treating others poorly, their accomplishments are not sustainable. Anyone can achieve *short-term* results by forcing compliance or mistreating others. However, if we want to attain *long-term* success, we must master the art of creating and nurturing relationships with key stakeholders—whether they are colleagues, employees or customers. Only then will we have a culture that honors the "how" along with the "what."

The third R (Renewal) consists of professional objectives that allow employees to "sharpen their saw" and learn new skills. By formalizing this third category, we reinforced that we expected all employees to focus on new skills and experiences designed to renew and expand their contributions to the organization. We asked each employee to commit to one or more professional development objectives that their manager could track throughout the year.

The Three Rs system proved to be incredibly effective for our organization. I encourage you to develop objectives in these three categories for your team. By focusing on Results, Relationships and Renewal, you can establish a balanced, comprehensive set of objectives for your people and measure their success throughout the year.

21) Establish Objectives that Focus on Results, Relationships and Renewal **22) Delegate Authority, Not Responsibility**
23) Promote Healthy Conflict 24) Provide Feedback at the "Teachable Moment" 25) Realize That Past Performance Is No Guarantee
of Future Results 26) Hold Yourself Accountable 27) Defeat Complacency 28) Communicate Clearly and Often
29) Listen Actively 30) Develop Other Leaders

CHAPTER
22

Delegate Authority, Not Responsibility

Fit leaders know they can increase their overall impact by leveraging the talents of their team members. The organizational reach of a leader often grows in direct proportion to her ability to delegate.

Unfortunately, many leaders find it difficult to let go of projects their team members could perform. Here are some common reasons leaders give for not delegating:

- There's no one I can trust.
- There's no time to delegate.
- I can't give away important tasks.
- It takes too long to explain.
- I can do it better and quicker myself.

Try to look past these excuses to start delegating. The stronger and more capable your employees, the more you can rely on them to help you accomplish your work. Focus on increasing the length of your "go-to" list of trusted employees. Not only will you develop the capabilities of your team members—you'll also prepare your people for more responsible positions.

If you want to become a master delegator, ask yourself these questions:

DELEGATION EXERCISE

- What stands in your way of delegating more?

- How long is your "short list" of people you go to on a routine basis to get things done?

- How deep is your bench of talented leaders ready to take on more senior-level assignments?

- What projects are you currently working on that can be delegated to others?

- What important work is not receiving your attention because of your continued involvement with work that can be handled by others?

See page 165 for exercise worksheet.

Train, Transfer and Track with a Delegation Diary

As leaders, we delegate to increase the total amount of work we can accomplish. By working with and through our team members, we not only achieve our goals more quickly and effectively—we also help our employees learn and grow. Unfortunately, many leaders struggle when it comes to delegating.

If you are having a tough time in the delegation department, think about the three T's: Train, Transfer and Track. Here's how it breaks down:

Train

When you hesitate to delegate to a team member, it's often because you worry the employee has not been properly trained. You are not alone—this "lack of training" fear is one of the most common barriers to delegation. However, as a leader, it's *your* responsibility to train your people. You have to teach them how to accomplish their work and successfully contribute to your team and organization.

When you do not take the time to train your employees, they feel underutilized and overlooked. They might wonder why you continue to pass them over as they see you continually hand out projects to the same small group of employees.

Of course, training an employee means you'll have to take time out of your busy schedule and teach him how to effectively perform important tasks. However, your efforts will pay off in the long run. If you spend some time training an employee upfront, you'll save countless hours when the time comes to transfer projects to him.

Transfer

When you delegate a project to a team member, you are not relinquishing responsibility. After all, your boss will continue to hold you accountable for accomplishing the ultimate business result.

Consequently, when you delegate you are essentially "deputizing" a member of your team. You are transferring your authority to her so she can act on your behalf in managing a project to completion. This allows you to focus your energies on other projects, knowing that members of your team are working to complete the tasks you've assigned to them.

21) Establish Objectives that Focus on Results, Relationships and Renewal 22) Delegate Authority, Not Responsibility
23) Promote Healthy Conflict 24) Provide Feedback at the "Teachable Moment" 25) Realize That Past Performance Is No Guarantee
of Future Results 26) Hold Yourself Accountable 27) Defeat Complacency 28) Communicate Clearly and Often
29) Listen Actively 30) Develop Other Leaders

Track

Once you've delegated a project to a team member, you cannot simply check it off your list and forget about it. Because you will remain responsible for the final outcome of the project, it is crucial to keep track of the employee's progress.

When I worked at Ford Motor Company, my supervisor kept track of all the projects he delegated by recording them in a notebook he kept in the top middle drawer of his desk. I came to refer to this sacred notebook as his "delegation diary." Because he documented all the projects he assigned to team members in this notebook, he had one central place where he could keep track of all of his outstanding delegations.

My supervisor would consult his delegation diary on a daily basis to determine if he needed to check in with an employee on the status of a particular project. While he was not a micromanager, he knew the value of stopping by at least a couple of times before the assignment was due. This gave him an opportunity to see if there were any unanticipated issues that might prevent the employee from delivering the project on time.

If you want to be a fit, effective leader, it's important to learn how to delegate. Remember, delegation is as easy as the three T's: Train, Transfer and Track. And never underestimate the value of a delegation diary!

CHAPTER
23

Promote Healthy Conflict

Fit leaders view conflict as an important path to personal *and* organizational growth. When they find themselves in disagreement with others, they remain open to reevaluating their own positions and perspectives. Always focused on how they can make things better, faster or more effective, fit leaders are dedicated to continuous improvement.

Many professionals go out of their way to avoid conflict at any cost—despite the fact that conflict often promotes a healthy exchange of alternative points of view. When you promote healthy conflict, you create powerful discussions among your team. This allows you to uncover multiple options before you choose the best course of action.

Do you run from conflict or encourage it? Ask yourself these questions:

HEALTHY CONFLICT EXERCISE

- How do you encourage powerful discussion and debate during team meetings?

- How consensual are you?

- What do you do to avoid becoming defensive when confronting objections to your plans?

- What techniques do you use to encourage participation by everyone during a meeting?

- How do you keep track of the different possibilities generated by your team?

See page 166 for exercise worksheet.

21) Establish Objectives that Focus on Results, Relationships and Renewal 22) Delegate Authority, Not Responsibility
23) Promote Healthy Conflict 24) Provide Feedback at the "Teachable Moment" 25) Realize That Past Performance Is No Guarantee
of Future Results 26) Hold Yourself Accountable 27) Defeat Complacency 28) Communicate Clearly and Often
29) Listen Actively 30) Develop Other Leaders

IN THE REAL WORLD

The Magic of Conflict

Do you see conflict as bad—as something that you want to run away from? Do you often see conflict as a contest over who is right and who is wrong?

When I ask my workshop participants to free associate with the word "conflict," these are the most frequently cited answers I hear:

- Anger
- Disagreement
- Frustration
- Dispute

- Tense
- Awkward
- Competition
- Difficult

- Two-sided
- Stress
- Violence
- Argumentative

The common thread weaving through all of these answers is negativity. Based on our personal experiences, many of us expect conflict to be hard and painful. However, the more we study what makes leaders effective and organizations successful, the more we realize that conflict does not have to be a negative experience. In fact, if you study how Mother Nature utilizes conflict, you will quickly see conflict as a force of positive change and beauty.

Have you ever been to the Grand Canyon in Arizona? If not, this sight is a must-see during your lifetime. I'm sure you've heard that no picture does justice to the real natural wonder. Believe it or not, the Grand Canyon was formed by conflict. The waters of the Colorado River crashed against the canyon mountains for hundreds of years, causing extensive erosion—which eventually created the Grand Canyon.

What about diamonds? Again, these beautiful gems are created through conflict. Diamonds are produced when coal is placed under intense pressure for many years. Finally, there is the sought after pearl. Pearls are the result of another form of conflict: irritation caused by sand inside an oyster shell.

Conflict has also led to the formation of many new governments over the last several hundred years. The USA is one example of an entirely new form of government created by conflict. Remember the Boston Tea Party?

The bottom line is this: It is inevitable that we will all face conflict in our lives. In fact, most of us confront some sort of conflict on a daily basis. However, if we learn to accept conflict and stay focused on the positive changes it can bring, we can transform it into a powerful and effective leadership asset.

CHAPTER 24

Provide Feedback at the "Teachable Moment"

Fit leaders boost the effectiveness of their teams by providing direct and timely feedback to team members. This creates an environment where employees always know whether their performance aligns with expectation.

As a fit leader, use feedback to:

- Recognize and reinforce an employee's areas of strength
- Identify areas for an employee's growth and development
- Indicate and quantify when an employee's performance is not acceptable

You will have the greatest impact on your employee's future performance if you provide feedback at the "teachable moment," right after the triggering event. If you want to increase your team's effectiveness by providing clear feedback, ask yourself the following questions:

FEEDBACK EXERCISE

- When was the last time you offered positive feedback to an employee?

- When you choose not to provide feedback to others, who steps in to do this for you?

- How do you utilize positive and constructive feedback to develop team members?

- When providing feedback, how important is it to address how the employee's behavior is impacting your team, the organization and customers?

- How do you follow-up with employees after you've given them feedback?

See page 167 for exercise worksheet.

21) Establish Objectives that Focus on Results, Relationships and Renewal 22) Delegate Authority, Not Responsibility
23) Promote Healthy Conflict **24) Provide Feedback at the "Teachable Moment"** 25) Realize That Past Performance Is No Guarantee
of Future Results 26) Hold Yourself Accountable 27) Defeat Complacency 28) Communicate Clearly and Often
29) Listen Actively 30) Develop Other Leaders

IN THE REAL WORLD

Our Seven-Step Process
for Giving Constructive Feedback

When leaders give feedback, they usually do not follow any kind of structured process to direct their discussion with the employee. If you often struggle with these awkward feedback conversations, our seven-step process can help.

In the Fit Leader's Program™ and Fit Leaders Academy, I teach a module called "The Gift of Feedback." During this session, I show leaders how to use the following seven-step constructive feedback process. (See checklist, page 84)

This seven-step process can greatly increase your confidence and effectiveness as you offer feedback to an employee. Here is how the checklist breaks down:

Step 1 Describe the Performance Problem

Simply describe the problem in a sentence or two. Try to remain as objective as possible and stick to one point—do not talk about multiple performance issues. Here's an example:

"Tom, I'd like to talk with you this afternoon because I've noticed that you've been late to four of our last five meetings."

Here you state the performance problem in a concise, simple-to-understand fashion. There should be no ambiguity as to why you're having this conversation with your team member.

Step 2 Explain the Impact of the Performance Problem

During feedback discussions, leaders often jump from the description of the problem directly to the development of an action plan. They want to know immediately what the employee is going to do to resolve the problem. However, I believe for a feedback conversation to be effective, it's important to first explain the *impact* of the employee's performance problem. This is the second step.

During this step, you help the employee understand how his behavior is impacting his colleagues, the organization and perhaps his customers. Let's go back to the previous example:

"Tom, I'd like to talk with you this afternoon because I've noticed that you've been late to four of our last five meetings. When you are late, it causes us to have to stop what we're doing while everyone acknowledges your arrival, and it interrupts the momentum of our meeting and lowers our productivity."

This second step is very important because many times the employee doesn't even realize his behavior causes a negative impact. If you don't describe how his behavior affects others, he might quickly dismiss the problem, saying something like, "Yeah, so what's your point? A lot of other people are late, too."

So, rather than just talking about the problem of being late, help him understand the impact he's having by being late. It's not just the lateness we're talking about, it's the diminished productivity, the lack of momentum, the interruption—and some might even say it's the dishonoring of the punctuality of the other people who arrived on time.

Here's another example:

"Jen, I wanted to talk with you today because I've noticed that you are the first to dismiss the ideas of other members of our team. Before you ask questions and try to understand someone else's position, you immediately point out how it won't work."

That's the problem. The impact might be as follows:

"When you are so quick to judge, it causes other members of the team to withdraw and withhold their input because they are afraid that when they speak you're going to cut them off or give all the reasons why their idea is stupid. And that works against the environment I'm trying to create where everyone feels comfortable sharing their unique perspectives."

Step 3   Identify the Cause of the Performance Problem

Once you have described the problem and explained the impact, then you can work with the employee to identify the cause of his performance problem. Let the employee take the lead here. Your job is to ask good open-ended questions that invite him to think about what might be causing his lateness—or what might be preventing her from listening before she shoots down a teammate's idea.

Don't jump in and immediately propose what you believe is causing the problem. You want the employee to really think on his own about the potential cause. Of course, you can certainly add your own view, especially if you think the employee is missing the real reason. But don't lead with your answer. Try to engage the employee with this conversation.

Step 4   Develop an Action Plan for Improving Performance

You can develop a much more valuable action plan once you've clearly described the problem, explained the impact and identified the cause. Now, you're likely to create an action plan that is focused on the real issue. If you sim-

21) Establish Objectives that Focus on Results, Relationships and Renewal 22) Delegate Authority, Not Responsibility
23) Promote Healthy Conflict **24) Provide Feedback at the "Teachable Moment"** 25) Realize That Past Performance Is No Guarantee
of Future Results 26) Hold Yourself Accountable 27) Defeat Complacency 28) Communicate Clearly and Often
29) Listen Actively 30) Develop Other Leaders

ply leap from performance problem to action plan, you miss out on a lot of conversation that might help you customize the specific elements of an action plan.

In step four, you're looking for the employee to commit to doing something different. Ask the employee what he can do to ensure he's able to attend meetings on time or what she can do to take time to listen to her colleagues' ideas before jumping in and being negative. Identify a solution, come up with a time table, make sure the action plan is specific and measurable and then agree on when you're going to follow up on these actions.

Step 5 Confirm Understanding

Before the conversation ends, ensure that both you and your employee are on the same page. This is an opportunity for you or the employee to summarize what was discussed, who has agreed to what, and when you're going to expect these changes to occur. If there is any disconnect, you can identify it during this conversation—not two weeks or a month down the road when you expect something to be done and then realize you misunderstood each other.

Step 6 Document the Conversation

I recommend that you document the conversation even if this is the first time you've had to talk with an employee about an issue—and *certainly* if it's the second time you're having the same conversation. For me, when something happens twice, it's a pattern. When you document it, you'll have the information available should this develop into a more serious performance management issue.

Step 7 Follow-up to Ensure Satisfactory Performance

More than likely, you or your employee will make some kind of commitment during the feedback conversation. It's incredibly important to follow up on these commitments. This helps you determine if the employee has actually improved or changed his behavior.

This seven-step checklist is a sequential process—you can't complete step two before you finish step one and so on. Walk through this checklist one step at a time. By following this process, you'll be more confident and effective at providing important feedback to others, and you'll feel more in control of the conversation.

Constructive Feedback Process Checklist

Instructions: Use the checklist below to plan, conduct, and follow-up with your constructive feedback discussion.

Constructive Feedback Process Strategies	Yes	No
Step 1 – Describe the Performance Problem		
1. Use objective terms that describe where, when, what, how much, or with whom.	☐	☐
2. Stay focused; stick to the point at hand.	☐	☐
3. Be brief; keep it short.	☐	☐
4. Keep it simple; use clear and concrete language.	☐	☐
Step 2 – Explain the Impact of the Performance Problem		
1. Describe how the performance is impacting the work team, the organization, or the customer.	☐	☐
2. Relate the performance problem to the employee's own target competencies and goals.	☐	☐
Step 3 – Identify the Cause of the Performance Problem		
1. Avoid language that appears to be blaming the employee.	☐	☐
2. Use open-ended questions to engage the employee.	☐	☐
3. Listen carefully to responses.	☐	☐
4. Refocus the discussion, as necessary.	☐	☐
5. Offer your view of causes if different than the employee's.	☐	☐
Step 4 – Develop an Action Plan for Improving Performance		
1. Keep the discussion focused on the future.	☐	☐
2. Agree to specific, observable, tangible results and/or outcomes.	☐	☐
3. Ask the employee for possible solutions.	☐	☐
4. Offer your ideas after you hear what your employee has to say.	☐	☐
5. Agree to a plan of action.	☐	☐
6. Agree to a follow-up date.	☐	☐
Step 5 - Confirm Understanding		
1. Agree on a specific course of action including timeframe.	☐	☐
2. Express confidence in the employee.	☐	☐
3. Thank the employee for his or her contributions.	☐	☐
Step 6 – Document the Conversation		
1. Document conversation on a separate piece of paper. Include the following information: a. Name of employee b. Description of performance problem c. Date of feedback discussion d. Brief summary of what occurred at each step e. Employee's comments f. Next steps	☐	☐
Step 7 – Follow-up to Ensure Satisfactory Performance		
1. Complete actions you agreed to take.	☐	☐
2. Check on the employee's progress.	☐	☐
3. Congratulate the employee if his or her performance improves.	☐	☐
4. Take additional action if performance does not improve.	☐	☐

CHAPTER
25

Realize That Past Performance Is No Guarantee of Future Results

It is not uncommon for newly-hired executives to bring former colleagues on board. In fact, this feels quite natural to many leaders. However, effective leaders understand that past achievements do not guarantee future success.

For example, say a new VP decides to hire an executive from her former organization. Because they worked together in the past, the VP is probably extremely comfortable with her former colleague. While she might expect this hiring decision to produce exceptional results for her new organization, this may not be the case.

A newly hired executive often encounters many hurdles. Some of these obstacles may seem impossible to overcome, leading the new recruit to feel disillusioned. If this disillusionment turns to despair, or even worse to "disconnect," the new hire will probably not make the contributions you might have expected when you hired him.

If you are considering bringing a former colleague into your new organization, ask yourself the following questions:

FUTURE RESULTS EXERCISE

- How likely is it that this executive will succeed in the new environment?

- What kind of disruption might you cause by bringing someone in from the outside?

- What type of assimilation coaching will you provide to ease his transition?

- What are your true motives for wanting a former colleague to join you in this new organization?

- How long can you wait for this executive to get up to speed?

See page 168 for exercise worksheet.

The Kiss of Death for New Leaders

As I've worked with many leaders who were recruited into new organizations, I've found that it's always a challenge to assimilate a new leader or general manager into a business. One of the greatest challenges for a new leader is to work with her new team in a way that honors their experience and the direction of the organization before she shares her vision for the team.

When leaders enter a new organization, they often make statements like, "In my experience, this is what works best," or worse yet, "In my old organization, we did it this way." I have found this to be the kiss of death for most new leaders. When you join a new organization, most people do not want to hear how you did it in your old organization. They are thinking, "This is not your old organization—this is *our* organization."

You can certainly share information about your former experiences, but share it in a way that doesn't point back to your former company. Remember that what worked well for you in your old organization may not work well for you in your new organization.

If you have recently joined a new organization, you may find it helpful to spend a couple of days trying to understand your team's needs and challenges. In fact, a process that I have used very successfully with new teams is to take them offsite for two days. I start this two-day offsite retreat by asking everyone in the room to think ahead three years. This is a conversation I learned in Dan Sullivan's Strategic Coach® Program.

Here's how it works: If it's February 11, 2022, I would say, "Today is February 11, 2022, and we're looking back on the last three years. What would've had to happen in those last three years for us to feel like we really made a difference—like we really succeeded in achieving the goals and objectives and strategies of our team?"

We spend time spelling out the things that would have to have happened for us to be able to look back and say, "Wow, what a wonderful three-year period that was. Look at everything we've accomplished."

21) Establish Objectives that Focus on Results, Relationships and Renewal 22) Delegate Authority, Not Responsibility
23) Promote Healthy Conflict 24) Provide Feedback at the "Teachable Moment" **25) Realize That Past Performance Is No Guarantee
of Future Results** 26) Hold Yourself Accountable 27) Defeat Complacency 28) Communicate Clearly and Often
29) Listen Actively 30) Develop Other Leaders

Once we figure out our vision, I ask the new team three more questions:

1. What are the dangers or barriers we're going to have to overcome to achieve that future result? What might get in the way of our future vision?

2. What are some of the opportunities we can take advantage of that will help us move in this direction?

3. What are our team's strengths, capabilities or core competencies that give us the confidence that we can achieve this vision?

So, first we take the time to develop a shared vision of the future. Then, we explore what will have to happen over the next three years to remove dangers, capitalize on opportunities and leverage our strengths to pull off this vision.

I have found that this process really brings a team together when a new leader joins the organization. By asking the questions described above, new leaders can properly assimilate into the new organization instead of just coming in and saying, "This is how I used to do it, so that's what we're going to do."

CHAPTER
26

Hold Yourself Accountable

Fit leaders follow through on their promises and commitments to others. They realize that finger pointing and playing the blame game is a waste of time and energy. Even when circumstances are less than desirable, leaders take responsibility for doing what is right.

If you want to develop personal accountability, start by asking yourself, "What can *I* do?" and "How can *I* make a difference?" Do not wait until someone tells you to do something—exercise initiative and ownership whenever you see an opportunity to add value.

Show your employees that you hold *yourself* accountable, and teach your team to avoid "playing the victim." Once your team members see that you hold yourself accountable, they will feel inspired and empowered to do the same.

Have you created an accountable culture for your team? Ask yourself the following questions:

ACCOUNTABILITY EXERCISE

- What is your track record when it comes to honoring your promises and commitments to others?

- How do you hold members of your team accountable for their commitments?

- When have you chosen excuses, whining or playing the victim instead of accountability?

- Where have you personally taken initiative in the last 90 days?

- What will you hold yourself and your team accountable for in the next 90 days?

See page 169 for exercise worksheet.

21) Establish Objectives that Focus on Results, Relationships and Renewal 22) Delegate Authority, Not Responsibility 23) Promote Healthy Conflict 24) Provide Feedback at the "Teachable Moment" 25) Realize That Past Performance Is No Guarantee of Future Results **26) Hold Yourself Accountable** 27) Defeat Complacency 28) Communicate Clearly and Often 29) Listen Actively 30) Develop Other Leaders

IN THE REAL WORLD

Choosing Accountability Over Victimhood

Accountability is about keeping our promises and owning our circumstances, no matter how unfavorable they may be. The opposite of accountability is "playing the victim." When they find themselves in an uncomfortable situation, many professionals position themselves as a victim, hoping this will absolve them of responsibility.

In *The Oz Principle* (Prentice Hall Press, 1998), authors Roger Connors, Tom Smith and Craig Hickman point to several ways people play the victim, including the following:

- Ignore/deny
- It's not my job
- Finger pointing
- Confusion/tell me what to do
- Cover your tail
- Wait and see

Let's explore how one of these victim approaches, ignore and deny, can prevent professionals from choosing the accountable path and leading effectively.

One cold January morning in 1986, I remember working my way through the cafeteria line at Ford Motor Company World Headquarters when we learned of the Challenger tragedy. As an avid follower of the space program, I was devastated by the news of the space shuttle explosion and the death of all seven astronauts aboard.

It was soon determined that the rubber O-rings, which had been designed to separate sections of the rocket booster during ascent, had failed due to cold temperatures on the morning of the launch. Some engineers at Morton Thiokol, the manufacturer of the O-rings, along with certain NASA employees, unsuccessfully tried to cancel the launch that day due to the unusually cold temperatures. They warned NASA leaders about the possibility of O-ring failure. Despite these concerns, NASA proceeded with the launch. The leaders in charge dismissed, ignored and denied the engineers' worst-case predictions.

If NASA leaders had studied the warnings from the engineers more closely, they could have averted the horrible disaster. NASA has since implemented several organizational changes designed to encourage greater communication across all levels and promote the acceptance of opposing points of view.

Let's consider another example of ignoring or denying facts as they accumulate: the 2005 Hurricane Katrina disaster. For more than a decade, researchers had been questioning the viability of the levees in place around New Orleans, arguing that they were not strong enough to protect the city from a serious hurricane. Study after study pointed to the structural weakness of the levees and predicted the current levees would fail against a Level 3 hurricane, let alone a Level 5 storm like Katrina.

Despite years of warnings, the city did not sufficiently shore up the levee system around New Orleans. Of course, we all know what happened when the levees failed—and many of us find ourselves asking why leaders failed to act sooner.

It takes courage to speak the truth—and it takes conviction to overcome all the pressures and self interests that work against taking a stand. However, effective leaders always choose to hold themselves accountable. While playing the victim may seem like the easier route, you can see in these two examples how ignoring and denying reality can lead to disastrous results. Leaders who choose to play the victim often pay a steep price in the end.

21) Establish Objectives that Focus on Results, Relationships and Renewal 22) Delegate Authority, Not Responsibility
23) Promote Healthy Conflict 24) Provide Feedback at the "Teachable Moment" 25) Realize That Past Performance Is No Guarantee
of Future Results 26) Hold Yourself Accountable **27) Defeat Complacency** 28) Communicate Clearly and Often
29) Listen Actively 30) Develop Other Leaders

CHAPTER
27

Defeat Complacency

Fit leaders establish a sense of urgency to defeat complacency and facilitate successful transitions. In his best-selling book *Leading Change* (Harvard Business Press, 1996), author John P. Kotter points to lack of urgency as one of the most significant factors in failed change efforts.

Even when a senior leadership team says they are on board with change, they often fail to build energy and win buy-in from the rest of the organization. According to Kotter, "Complacency with the status quo turns out to be a powerful barrier to change initiatives even when leaders confront it head on."

When organizations rest on their laurels, they become complacent. In fact, it is often the most successful enterprises that find themselves in this dangerous position. These companies expect that nothing will ever get in the way of their continued domination in the marketplace. Bolstered by their past successes and blinded by the illusion that nothing can touch them, these organizations convince themselves that change is not necessary.

Are you creating a sense of urgency for your team? Ask these questions:

COMPLACENCY EXERCISE

- How wed are you to the status quo?

- What information do you share with your team to keep them aware of both dangers and opportunities?

- How do you factor objective feedback into your decision making and planning process?

- How often do you use "happy talk" when communicating organizational challenges?

- What are you doing to defeat complacency in your organization?

See page 170 for exercise worksheet.

IN THE REAL WORLD

Overcoming Resistance

Like the human body, an organization has a well-developed immune system designed to protect against external invaders and maintain the status quo. In the case of the human body, foreign intruders are usually germs—but in organizations, the "intruders" are often new ideas, programs and people.

Consequently, when a leader sponsors a change initiative, he will almost certainly encounter some resistance from his team. In fact, you may assume something is wrong if your team *doesn't* resist change. If everyone immediately jumps on board with your new idea or program, you may want to question whether you are pushing the envelope far enough.

Although all leaders expect to face some pushback when introducing change, many of us don't know how to handle the resistance. Here are a few proven strategies to help you overcome or neutralize your team's resistance:

The "20-50-30" Rule

When it comes to leading change, you can expect that roughly 20 percent of your people will generally resist any new idea or approach. If you're like countless other leaders, you probably spend way too much of your precious time trying to convince this group to get on board—even though experience suggests that this fifth of your organization will remain unconvinced and simply try to drag you down.

In most organizations, the next 50 percent of people are neutral or what we might call "fence sitters" when it comes to change. They will look around and wait to see how others react. If the people around them sign up for the change, they are likely to quickly follow.

The final 30 percent represents the change-friendly population who are usually the quickest to accept change. By focusing your efforts on the 30 percent that are change-friendly and the 50 percent that are open to change, you can optimize your success rate in implementing any change initiative. However, if you focus too much of your time on the first 20 percent, you take your eye off the majority of people who are most likely to help you implement the change.

21) Establish Objectives that Focus on Results, Relationships and Renewal 22) Delegate Authority, Not Responsibility 23) Promote Healthy Conflict 24) Provide Feedback at the "Teachable Moment" 25) Realize That Past Performance Is No Guarantee of Future Results 26) Hold Yourself Accountable **27) Defeat Complacency** 28) Communicate Clearly and Often 29) Listen Actively 30) Develop Other Leaders

Share the Rationale

You can also overcome resistance by explaining the rationale for the change to your team. People often respond more positively to a transition when they understand the context or reason for the change. Because the reason is so clear in your own head, you might assume that everyone around you understands the rationale for the change. Don't make this mistake. If you take time to help others see how the change will solve current problems and ensure a better future, your team members are more likely to align with this new path.

Focus on the "Me" Issues

As you present a change to your team, try to take care of the "me" issues. In other words, help your employees understand how the change will impact their jobs, their roles and their day-to-day activities. When people are left to speculate what a change means for them personally, they usually just make it up themselves. Unfortunately, people tend to fill in the blanks with scenarios that are often far more negative than what is likely to occur. If you take some time upfront to explain the change and the ways it will impact them, you'll remove a lot of the uncertainty.

Promise Problems

When it comes to introducing new programs, many champions of change over promise and under deliver. They sugarcoat anticipated roadblocks and try to convince people that the change process will be a piece of cake.

A more effective approach is to promise problems. Let your team know that the change will be tough and you will all get through it together. If the journey ends up being easier than you communicated, your team will feel energized by getting through the change with less pain than expected. If that's the case, you will have under promised and over delivered—a much better outcome for change leaders.

CHAPTER
28

Communicate Clearly and Often

Fit leaders know how to communicate effectively with their teams. The most successful leaders realize their team members thrive on certain types of communication—while other types of communication cause their employees' engagement and trust to wane.

You can probably think of a few specific examples when you have communicated in ways that were uplifting for your people. On the other hand, you can probably also think of a few times when you communicated in ways that sapped the energy of your team or took their focus off of what was most important.

If you want to be an effective leader, try to communicate clearly and often, embrace the kind of communication that inspires and motivates your employees, and steer clear of the types of communication that bore or frustrate them. Reinforce your messages by using repetition and leverage multiple platforms and media.

Are you communicating effectively with your team? Ask yourself the following questions:

EFFECTIVE COMMUNICATION EXERCISE

- What are the different ways that you communicate with your team?

- How do you know when your communication is ineffective?

- What types of communication do you prefer from others?

- How do you communicate team priorities in a way that aligns people with what is most important to them and the organization?

- How do you ensure that your communication is timely?

See page 171 for exercise worksheet.

21) Establish Objectives that Focus on Results, Relationships and Renewal 22) Delegate Authority, Not Responsibility 23) Promote Healthy Conflict 24) Provide Feedback at the "Teachable Moment" 25) Realize That Past Performance Is No Guarantee of Future Results 26) Hold Yourself Accountable 27) Defeat Complacency **28) Communicate Clearly and Often** 29) Listen Actively 30) Develop Other Leaders

The Communication Your Employees Want

Over the years, I have asked thousands of workshop participants what kind of communication they want and expect from their leaders, and I consistently receive the same answers. Employees say they seek communication that is:

- Straightforward and direct
- Comprehensive
- Clear and concise
- Positive
- Constructive
- Timely and specific
- Frequent
- Face-to-face when appropriate
- Professional
- Big picture
- Two-way
- Informative about the company's performance

On the other hand, participants say they *don't* appreciate the following types of communication from their leaders:

- Too much information
- Rambling
- Non-actionable feedback
- Company gossip
- Unjustified interruptions
- Non-constructive criticism
- Condescension
- Micromanagement
- Negative attitudes
- Constant changes in direction
- Lack of support or commitment
- Vagueness
- Finger pointing
- Passing the buck
- Conflicting goals and priorities
- Over-communication

If you want to be an effective communicator, put your presentations, speeches and casual business conversations to the test. Does your communication include all the qualities from the first list? Do you find yourself slipping in any of the negative qualities from the second list?

As you speak to your team, take note of the kinds of communication that seem to energize and motivate them. Consider asking your team members or other colleagues for honest feedback on your communication skills. After all, most of us have blind spots that will come to light only through the lenses and experiences of those with whom we communicate on a regular basis.

CHAPTER
29

Listen Actively

Fit leaders communicate effectively because they have mastered the art of active listening. They are not only adept at sending clear, unambiguous messages—they also excel at receiving them.

Leaders sometimes allow distractions, attitudes or personal biases to interfere with their ability to engage in a beneficial listening experience. Instead of hearing things the way they are, they hear things the way they *think* they are. This "judgmental awareness" can get in the leader's way and distort the speaker's intended messages.

To become an active listener, it's important to focus on the person speaking to you. Encourage her train of thought by listening intently without interruption. Once she is finished, communicate that you are actively listening by restating and summarizing her key points.

If you want to be an active listener and masterful communicator, ask yourself the following questions:

ACTIVE LISTENING EXERCISE

- How do you feel when someone else is not truly listening to you?

- How often do you catch yourself rushing to formulate your next response while the other person is still speaking?

- How will the quality of your relationships be affected by more active listening on your part?

- What will it take for you to finish listening before you begin speaking?

- How will you change your personal listening experience to make it more fulfilling?

See page 172 for exercise worksheet.

21) Establish Objectives that Focus on Results, Relationships and Renewal 22) Delegate Authority, Not Responsibility
23) Promote Healthy Conflict 24) Provide Feedback at the "Teachable Moment" 25) Realize That Past Performance Is No Guarantee
of Future Results 26) Hold Yourself Accountable 27) Defeat Complacency 28) Communicate Clearly and Often
29) Listen Actively 30) Develop Other Leaders

10 Irritating Listening Habits

As we all know, it's easy to *pretend* to listen to a speaker. However, when you actively listen to your team members, colleagues and customers, not only will you learn so much more from the conversation—you'll also nurture crucial relationships.

How many times have you tried to discuss an important issue with a colleague only to have him rudely interrupt you in the middle of your thought process? Have you ever tried to talk to someone who seems to be looking everywhere except at you? Have you encountered one of those annoying people who always has a story that "tops" your story? If you answered yes to any of these questions, you know just how frustrating it can be to talk to a bad listener.

Unfortunately, many leaders are guilty of these same terrible listening practices. If you want to be an active listener, try to avoid these top ten irritating listening habits:

1. Interrupting the speaker.
2. Not looking at the speaker.
3. Rushing the speaker and making her feel that she's wasting your time.
4. Showing interest in something other than the conversation.
5. Getting ahead of the speaker and finishing his thoughts.
6. Not responding to the speaker's requests.
7. Saying "Yes, but..." as if you have made up your mind.
8. Topping the speaker's story with "That reminds me..." or "That's nothing, let me tell you about..."
9. Forgetting what you talked about previously.
10. Asking too many questions about details.

Also, remember to let silence do the heavy lifting. Too often, we are afraid of silence when we communicate with others. If you ask a question and the speaker doesn't answer immediately, don't jump right in with your own answer or try a different version of your question. Allow the other person enough time and space to think about your question before answering. If you rush in to cover up the silence, you may eliminate the possibility of getting an authentic answer from the other person. In a way, silence is a form of listening.

CHAPTER
30

Develop Other Leaders

Fit leaders invest time in identifying and developing potential successors. They regularly chart the strengths, needs and improvement opportunities of promising professionals within their organizations.

If you want to create sustainability and build long-term value for your company, it's important to make sure your organization's top talent receives attention, rotational assignments and other developmental opportunities to keep them engaged and committed. Plus, by taking the time to map talent within your company, you ensure that successor candidates are prepared when promotional opportunities arise.

Complete the succession chart below and make a point to update it regularly.

Your Succession Chart

	E Emergency	RN Ready Now	RT Ready in Time	RLT Ready Long Term
Your Job				
Critical Job #1:				
Critical Job #2:				
Critical Job #3:				

E = Emergency
Who can step into the position now even though they are not entirely ready?

• _____

• _____

RN = Ready Now (within 1 year)
Whom do you expect to be ready in less than a year?

• _____

• _____

RT = Ready in Time (within 1-3 Years)
Who will be ready to step in after additional development?

• _____

• _____

RLT = Ready Long Term (>3 years)
In whom do you see potential on a longer-term basis?

• _____

• _____

21) Establish Objectives that Focus on Results, Relationships and Renewal 22) Delegate Authority, Not Responsibility
23) Promote Healthy Conflict 24) Provide Feedback at the "Teachable Moment" 25) Realize That Past Performance Is No Guarantee
of Future Results 26) Hold Yourself Accountable 27) Defeat Complacency 28) Communicate Clearly and Often
29) Listen Actively **30) Develop Other Leaders**

Are you taking time to develop other leaders? Ask yourself these questions:

LEADER DEVELOPMENT EXERCISE

- Who are your high-performing employees?

- What process do you have in place to regularly review the talent in your organization?

- What are you doing to retain your best people?

- What positions on your team are crucial to achieving your current and future business goals?

- What legacy do you seek to leave?

See page 173 for exercise worksheet.

Preparing for Tomorrow

Most leaders spend countless hours reviewing their quarterly financial performance, new product plans, inventory levels and other dashboard-driven business data. Oddly enough, many of these same leaders neglect to conduct a periodic formal review of their human resources.

Many years ago, I created a Talent Review Program for my organization. This program ensured that leaders set time aside to regularly review each employee's strengths, needs and improvement opportunities. Managers were required to conduct this review for each of their employees every six to 12 months.

During these talent reviews, the senior executive of each operating unit met with the CEO and the senior human resources executive to discuss the developmental status of each of their employees. They focused on ensuring the organization's best people were receiving the attention, rotational assignments and other developmental opportunities to keep them engaged and committed. The process also helped our management team identify talent-ready employees—so when a new opportunity arose, the management team could assign it to the appropriate person.

This talent review program also allowed leaders to identify employees not performing up to expectation. They would decide whether to develop an improvement plan and coach these employees to higher performance levels or remove the poor performing employees from the organization.

Most talent review programs ask leaders to rank their employees using two or three categories, such as High Potential, High Performing and Performance Problem. I decided to include a couple more categories to drive distinctions among different levels of performance and opportunity.

In my program, I use the following five-category scale:
1. High Potential
2. High Performer
3. Solid Performer
4. Question Mark
5. Move Out

21) Establish Objectives that Focus on Results, Relationships and Renewal 22) Delegate Authority, Not Responsibility
23) Promote Healthy Conflict 24) Provide Feedback at the "Teachable Moment" 25) Realize That Past Performance Is No Guarantee
of Future Results 26) Hold Yourself Accountable 27) Defeat Complacency 28) Communicate Clearly and Often
29) Listen Actively **30) Develop Other Leaders**

Here is how each category breaks down:

High Potential employees have the capability to take on an executive leadership role in the organization at some point in the future. By designating an employee as High Potential, we are saying we believe this individual has both the ability and the aspiration to rise to a senior position. One day, these employees will be ready to take over our jobs on the senior team.

We want to make sure we are moving High Potential employees along at the right pace. It's important to provide opportunities for them to learn as much about the organization as possible, perhaps by offering them rotations in other departments. Many leading companies move their highest potential people to positions around the nation, and oftentimes the world, to create the best-rounded executives.

High Performer employees consistently go above and beyond the call of duty when it comes to their work. They contribute at a high level and can be expected to deliver high quality work without excessive supervision. However, unlike High Potential employees, High Performers do not show signs of interest or capacity to step up into a senior leadership role.

High Performers are our go-to people for our most challenging assignments and opportunities, yet they don't quite have what we are looking for in the next generation of our leadership team. And that is okay. After all, there are only a handful of opportunities at the top, so not every High Performer will have a chance to rise to the highest levels of our organization. Still, we need to recognize High Performers for their stellar performance. It's important to compensate them well and offer them other benefits to show our appreciation for their great work.

Solid Performers are the backbone of most organizations, and we can count on them to reliably perform their duties. While Solid Performers don't consistently go above and beyond the call of duty like the High Performers, they do their jobs well and are responsible for much of the day-to-day activities in an organization.

Question Mark employees are not Solid Performers today, and they may be at risk for losing their jobs. In other words, the jury is still out on these employees. Senior managers need to assess Question Mark employees in real time and try to coach them to become Solid Performers by the next review period. If Question Mark employees show no improvement in their developmental issues, senior management may have to dismiss them from the organization.

It is important to point out that an employee may fall into the Question Mark category simply because he has just moved into a new role within the company. While he may have been a Solid Performer or even a High Performer in his previous role, he may be considered a Question Mark employee as senior managers wait to see if he proves successful in his new position. The talent review process is designed to be dynamic and applicable to an employee's entire career within an organization. Therefore, it is quite possible for an employee to move around from one category to the next within a relatively short amount of time. This is why it is important to assess and manage talent on a continuous basis.

Move Out employees have serious developmental needs. An employee who falls into this category has not been able to improve her skill set in a way that continues her relevance to the organization. The Move Out employee may also demonstrate certain negative behaviors or attitudes that contaminate her team.

Whatever the cause, these employees have two choices: They can rectify the situation or they must move out of the organization. Either way, senior leaders need to make a decision quickly. It's important to be proactive with the talent review process—and that means leaders must remove employees who do not "belong on the bus" in a timely fashion.

We've all seen what happens when an employee sticks around well beyond his usefulness. Leaders often ignore these poor performers or feel powerless to do anything about them. When incompetent employees remain in an organization, they use up scarce salary dollars that could be applied to securing higher-performing employees.

With a proactive talent review program in place, organizations shine a light on these ineffective employees and force leaders and managers to be accountable for the quality of their staff. The bottom line is this: When you have a strong talent review program in place, your company will be more powerful and effective. Not only will it encourage you to raise the bar for your employees, but it will also help you identify tomorrow's leaders.

PART 4

VITALITY

[The Fourth Face of Leadership Fitness]

VITALITY

An Introduction

As my model of leadership fitness was taking shape, I initially concluded that leaders could create a powerful impact by integrating just the three central qualities we've discussed so far: clarity, confidence and effectiveness. However, as I continued to explore what drives sustainable success, I discovered the model was missing a fourth critical ingredient: vitality.

Over the years, I have observed countless leaders who have failed to "go the distance." Many of these leaders appeared to be "fit" in every other way—they were clear, confident and effective. They set unambiguous objectives for their teams, they knew how to silence their inner gremlins, and they were highly effective managers. Yet, I watched these same leaders repeatedly grow frustrated, overwhelmed, overloaded and even physically ill. These leaders were unable to make a lasting impact because they eventually ran out of steam. Once I recognized this limitation, I knew I needed to add vitality to the model.

I see vitality as a measure of our energy, stamina and endurance. Leaders equipped with this powerful characteristic are masters at managing the numerous competing demands for their time. They know how to nurture their physical, emotional, mental and spiritual energy. They make better food choices, exercise regularly and take time off to rejuvenate and recharge their batteries.

I have come to believe that vitality is the most dynamic of all four qualities of leadership fitness—because without it, a leader cannot maintain the other three qualities. Without vitality, leaders struggle to achieve clarity. After all, mental acuity and physical vitality are closely linked. Without vitality, leaders have a difficult time remaining confident. And finally, without vitality, leaders quickly deplete the energy they need to lead effectively.

31) Strike a Balance Between Personal and Professional Obligations 32) Calendarize Commitments
33) Overcome Overwhelm 34) Exercise for Lifelong Health 35) Make Healthier Food Choices 36) Take Time Out
37) Manage Stress 38) Choose Optimism 39) Oscillate Between Periods of Work and Rest 40) Go the Distance

If you are seeking more vitality in your life, ask yourself these questions:

- What kind of balance do I have between my professional and personal life?

- How can I make my to-do list vanish every 24 hours?

- What can I do to avoid becoming overwhelmed?

- How often do I exercise?

- What kind of foods do I consume?

- When was the last time I took time out from work?

- How well do I manage stress?

- What can I do to be more optimistic?

- How can I alternate between periods of work and rest?

- How will I develop the stamina I need to go the distance?

In chapters 31 through 40, I will help you answer each of these questions and teach you how to develop vitality, the fourth and final face of leadership fitness.

If you want to be a fit leader, it's important to leverage the dynamic synergies between all four faces of leadership fitness. You will derive power and balance from the interrelationships between clarity, confidence, effectiveness and vitality. This will give you the staying power you need to reach the highest levels of leadership success.

CHAPTER
31

Strike a Balance
Between Personal and Professional Obligations

Fit leaders live whole and balanced lives. Although they commit great amounts of energy to pursuing their professional goals, they also maintain perspective about all the other important aspects of their lives. In other words, fit leaders do not focus solely on their career aspirations—they spend time enjoying and working on their personal lives, as well.

If you fall into a routine of working "all the time," you may begin to wonder how else you could possibly spend your days. Far too many leaders believe if they are not toiling away at the office or striving to reach their professional goals, they are simply wasting their time.

In order to develop vitality, it's crucial to discover alignment in your life—an equilibrium between your career, family and friends, your health and your financial well-being. If you want to strike a balance between your personal and professional obligations, start with an honest self-assessment of how you spend your time each day. Then, try to determine what changes you need to make to bring more balance to your life.

Do you need to realign your life with what really matters? Ask yourself the following questions.

LIFE BALANCE EXERCISE

- How satisfied are you with the balance in your life today?

- What areas of your life would benefit from greater attention?

- How often do you truly disconnect from your work?

- What is the one small step you might take this week to bring your life more into balance?

- How will you boost your balance in the next 90 days?

See page 176 for exercise worksheet.

31) Strike a Balance Between Personal and Professional Obligations 32) Calendarize Commitments
33) Overcome Overwhelm 34) Exercise for Lifelong Health 35) Make Healthier Food Choices 36) Take Time Out
37) Manage Stress 38) Choose Optimism 39) Oscillate Between Periods of Work and Rest 40) Go the Distance

How Bumpy Is Your Ride?

Your life is made up of many different parts—from your career and your family and friends to your health and your financial well-being. In fact, the average person has eight major life areas, as indicated in "The Wheel of Life" below. This excellent tool, which I first discovered during my coach training at The Coaches Training Institute, reveals the amount of balance you have in your life based on how you allocate your precious time.

You can measure your own life balance with this simple exercise. On the wheel below, treat the center as 0 and the outer edge as 10. Rank your current level of satisfaction with each slice of your life by drawing a straight or curved line to create a new outer edge.

If you believe you allocate the optimal amount of time in any of the eight wedges, simply draw over the line on the circle's outer edge. If you believe you are actually closer to a ranking of 5 for any given wedge, draw a new line between the center of the circle (which represents 0) and the outer circle (which represents 10). Feel free to draw your line anywhere between the center point and the outer edge of the circle to match your present level of satisfaction within each segment of the wheel.

The new perimeter represents the wheel of your life. If this were a real wheel, how bumpy would the ride be?

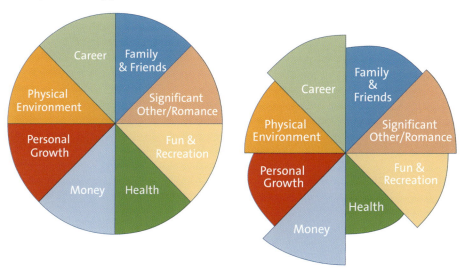

Based on your personal Wheel of Life, take some time to complete the following statements:

I will boost my balance by making the following changes in the **Family & Friends** *slice of my life:*
Example: I will call my brother at least once a month.

_____

_____

_____

I will boost my balance by making the following changes in the **Significant Other/ Romance** *slice of my life:*
Example: I will plan a "date night" with my significant other for every Thursday.

_____

_____

_____

I will boost my balance by making the following changes in the **Fun & Recreation** *slice of my life:*
Example: I will go fishing next week.

_____

_____

_____

I will boost my balance by making the following changes in the **Health** *slice of my life:*
Example: I will add two more exercise sessions to my routine each week.

_____

_____

_____

I will boost my balance by making the following changes in the **Money** *slice of my life:*
Example: I will create and stick to a monthly budget.

_____

_____

_____

31) Strike a Balance Between Personal and Professional Obligations 32) Calendarize Commitments
33) Overcome Overwhelm 34) Exercise for Lifelong Health 35) Make Healthier Food Choices 36) Take Time Out
37) Manage Stress 38) Choose Optimism 39) Oscillate Between Periods of Work and Rest 40) Go the Distance

I will boost my balance by making the following changes in the **Personal Growth** *slice of my life:*

Example: I will take a class this semester at the local community college.

I will boost my balance by making the following changes in the **Physical Environment** *slice of my life:*

Example: I will clean out my office this week.

I will boost my balance by making the following changes in the **Career** *slice of my life:*

Example: I will calendarize free days several times a month.

CHAPTER 32

Calendarize Commitments

Fit leaders recognize that one of the biggest drains on their vitality is the lack of control they often feel due to all of the promises and commitments they make on a daily basis. While a leader may create a "to-do" list to temporarily accumulate the commitments she makes during the day, she also develops a daily practice of managing her to-do list so each item vanishes before the start of a new day.

If you want to be a fit leader, it's important to process your entire to-do list at least once every 24 hours. The goal is to check every item off your list by performing one of the following three steps:

1. Do any task(s) that can be done in two minutes or less.
2. Delegate a task that does not require your personal involvement.
3. Dedicate a specific block of future time on your calendar when you can commit to working on the task. I call this "calendarizing."

Do you use your calendar as the principal organizing tool in your life? Ask yourself the following questions:

CALENDARIZING EXERCISE

- How long is your to-do list?

- What are the typical tasks you accumulate each day that can reasonably be completed in two minutes or less?

- What tasks are you holding onto that could safely be handled by others?

- How many times have you approached the deadline for a task for which you have not scheduled sufficient time to complete?

- How often do others in your organization place meetings on your calendar because your calendar shows open space when in fact you need to spend that time working on other commitments?

See page 177 for exercise worksheet.

31) Strike a Balance Between Personal and Professional Obligations **32) Calendarize Commitments**
33) Overcome Overwhelm 34) Exercise for Lifelong Health 35) Make Healthier Food Choices 36) Take Time Out
37) Manage Stress 38) Choose Optimism 39) Oscillate Between Periods of Work and Rest 40) Go the Distance

IN THE REAL WORLD

The Vanishing To-Do List™

Many people take great pride in being expert list-makers. Plagued by forgotten appointments, missed deadlines and an embarrassing lack of follow-up, many of us feel compelled at some point to start making lists. I count myself as one of the "list-making" pack. Many years ago when I started making lists, I took comfort in the knowledge that everything I needed to do was on some list…somewhere.

Therein lays the problem with lists: Most list-makers have multiple lists in numerous places. I know some people who spend hours upon hours just consolidating their lists. Then there are the folks who use multi-colored post-it notes or "stickies" to write down important information and reminders. Of course, when they need to refer back to information they've recorded on that bright pink sticky (or was it the blue one?), it takes them valuable minutes to locate the correct note. Usually, the note they are searching for is buried somewhere deep below other stacks of papers on their desk.

Finally, there are countless people who use those pesky Microsoft Outlook notifications. These folks are forever being "dinged" by reminders that some deadline is approaching or some call needs to be made or some meeting is about to start. These haphazard personal organization systems are ineffective at best and an even bigger distraction and a waste of precious time at worst.

So, where does the madness end? For me, it ended with The Vanishing To-Do List™. This productivity-boosting tool works exactly as it sounds. I utilize a single to-do list (just one), and all of the items on that list systematically disappear by the end of each day. Here's how it works:

Each day, I use my to-do list (I personally use the Reminders function on my iPhone) to accumulate the commitments I make, e.g., send an article to a client, develop a proposal for a leadership development workshop, place a follow-up call or order a book from Amazon.com. I can be in a meeting, on the phone or even hard at work at my desk when I think of something I want or need to do—but not right now. When this occurs, I simply add the item to my to-do list.

I have only one list, and all items, even more personal-related tasks and reminders (call Mom, buy a new tie, pick up a new hand tool, etc.), are placed into this single repository of follow-up activities. The beauty and logic of a single list is the ease of mind that comes from knowing all the important tasks I want to remember are always accessible in this one place.

For me, all I have to do is open the Reminders list on my hand-held device (which is automatically synched with my desktop computer version of Microsoft Outlook), and all of my to-dos are clearly visible. If a hard-copy day-planner works better for you, keep a single list you can turn to at any time and know that all of your to-do activities will be accessible there.

Now, here is where the vanishing part comes in. Before I retire each night, I make sure that nothing remains on my to-do list. The goal is to start fresh each day with a blank list. This is how I do it: I start at the top of my list and make a simple decision about what action I need to take to complete that first task. If I can do it quickly, usually in two minutes or less, I complete the task right then and there. So, for example, if one of the items on my list is to send an article or book reference to a client, I open up my email and immediately send the requested information. This takes less than two minutes to accomplish. After I email this information to my client, I return to my task list where I joyfully place a checkmark next to that first task.

Then, I move to the next item on my list. This next item could better be handled by my assistant. So, I simply send a quick email or handwrite a short note asking my assistant to set up a meeting or order a book or take care of whatever task it may be that she can more efficiently handle. After delegating the second item on my list, I place a checkmark next to that item. Two down, nine to go. The next item (prepare a proposal for a prospective client) cannot be completed in less than two minutes, and it is not an activity I can delegate to someone else. So, before I can place a checkmark next to this item, I need to actually schedule time on my calendar (for some time in the future) when I can dedicate time to complete this task.

Now this is critical! I never leave the item on my to-do list just because I do not have the time to complete it right then and there. Instead, I determine what I need to do to complete the task, and I "calendarize" the item so I have dedicated time (tomorrow, the next day, next week, etc.) to complete this task before it is due. In other words, I am reserving time in the future to complete an important task that otherwise would just remain on my to-do list and simply get moved from one day to the next.

It is too easy to keep avoiding the bigger tasks on our list if we don't commit to spending the necessary time to complete them in the future. For example, let's say you know you need a total of two days to prepare a presentation, and you keep putting this task off (and keep it on your list without ever doing anything about it). More than likely, you will get closer and closer to the

31) Strike a Balance Between Personal and Professional Obligations **32) Calendarize Commitments**
33) Overcome Overwhelm 34) Exercise for Lifelong Health 35) Make Healthier Food Choices 36) Take Time Out
37) Manage Stress 38) Choose Optimism 39) Oscillate Between Periods of Work and Rest 40) Go the Distance

date of your presentation and still not be ready. By then, you may have used all the open spaces on your calendar to commit to other activities—so in the end, you'll rush to put together a slapdash presentation that really deserved the two days you should have dedicated to it up front.

So, let's back up. Let's say you added the item "prepare a presentation" to your to-do list today. Rather than concluding that this can wait until next week, you determine that you need a total of two days to prepare. So, you schedule two hours on your calendar for later this week to outline the presentation. You schedule another half-day for sometime the following week to do some necessary research for your talk and begin organizing your thoughts. Finally, you schedule additional time on your calendar for a day the week before the actual presentation for editing, practicing and production of materials. You can then place a checkmark next to this item on your to-do list because you have "calendarized" this task. You have broken up this important project into its logical components and can rest easy knowing that you have allotted sufficient time on your calendar to get it done.

By following this method each night (or whenever your working day comes to an end), you can eliminate all items on your to-do list each day and start fresh with a new list the next morning. The Vanishing To-Do List allows you to confidently process all the items on your to-do list on a daily basis. I challenge you to try this technique for the next two weeks. Who knows? It may end up being the perfect personal organization system for you.

CHAPTER
33

Overcome Overwhelm

Fit leaders know how to conquer feelings of overwhelm. It's not unusual for a leader to feel inundated with tasks and stressed about everything he must get done—particularly as his list of responsibilities starts to grow. While most of us can comfortably handle a certain level of activity, we may find ourselves wondering how we are going to accomplish everything when we must take on new duties.

If you are feeling overwhelmed by your mounting responsibilities, increase your vitality by getting organized. Think about the last time you had a messy desk. How "in control" did you feel? As you peered down at a desk covered with piles of jumbled papers, memos and reminders, you probably felt frazzled, anxious and completely out of control. In other words, you felt overwhelmed. However, once you took a few minutes to organize and get your desk back in order, the tasks at hand seemed much more manageable.

Much like cleaning off your desk, you can regain control of your circumstances by using two powerful strategies: planning and delegation. If you plan ahead and delegate tasks on a regular basis, you will move from a situation where your job controls you to a situation where you control your job.

If you want to overcome overwhelm, ask yourself the following questions:

OVERWHELM EXERCISE

- On a scale of 1 to 10, with 10 being the highest, what is your present level of overwhelm?

- What are you doing to regain more control over your circumstances?

- How much time do you set aside on a weekly basis to plan what needs to get done?

- How can you leverage the skills and talents of others to complete your work?

- What can you do to avoid the frustration and sense of desperation that arises from having too much to do?

See page 178 for exercise worksheet.

31) Strike a Balance Between Personal and Professional Obligations 32) Calendarize Commitments
33) Overcome Overwhelm 34) Exercise for Lifelong Health 35) Make Healthier Food Choices 36) Take Time Out
37) Manage Stress 38) Choose Optimism 39) Oscillate Between Periods of Work and Rest 40) Go the Distance

IN THE REAL WORLD

Plan and Delegate to Defeat Overwhelm

There was a time in my career when my level of responsibility jumped significantly, literally overnight. I can still remember the overwhelming sense of desperation I felt for almost a week. A few times, I even thought about giving up on my newly acquired responsibilities so I could simply return to the "old normal." Fortunately, I did not take that route.

Instead, I learned the importance of dedicating time for planning and delegation. I realized that with new assignments comes the need to understand new issues, assess new people and chart new directions. Often, an overwhelmed leader will mistakenly put these vital tasks on the backburner as she continues to tread water, wondering how she is going to absorb all of the additional work. In the meantime, her energy is drained.

If you want to gain clarity in an unfamiliar or stressful situation, take time to identify key issues, important milestones and expectations. By planning ahead, you will significantly increase your sense of control. Once you know what needs to be accomplished in each of your areas of responsibility, you can determine which tasks you will need to handle personally and which ones you can delegate to others.

When you take on additional responsibilities, you may also take on a new team. Because you are unfamiliar with the skills your new employees have to offer, you may be tempted to take the "easy" way out and do everything your-self. If you choose this path, you will underutilize the talents of your team and increase your own level of stress. On the other hand, if you get up to speed as quickly as possible through the proper planning steps, you can confidently turn to others and seek their assistance in completing key elements of your plans.

It's easy to convince yourself that you must be the author of all new guide-lines, products, procedures and processes, but don't make this critical mistake. Not only will this contribute to your overwhelm—it will also slow everything down as you become a bottleneck.

Take the time to plan, and once you are clear about what needs to be done, delegate to engage others in important work. In doing so, you will assert more control over your expanding job, minimize your sense of overwhelm and preserve your vitality.

CHAPTER
34

Exercise for Lifelong Health

Fit leaders know that regular exercise is a critical part of staying productive and healthy. The U.S. Centers for Disease Control and Prevention (CDC) recommends that adults do at least 150 minutes of moderate-intensity aerobic activity each week.

Unfortunately, many leaders quickly grow bored or frustrated with their fitness regimen and eventually stop exercising altogether. If you are struggling to stick with a routine, remember the key is to find the type of exercise that will keep you motivated. For example, if you love spending time outdoors, try walking, running or biking. If you enjoy exercising with others, join a gym or an aerobics class. If you prefer working out alone, buy some fun fitness DVDs or consider investing in a treadmill, elliptical or stationery bike for your home. If you quickly lose interest in the same old exercises, hire a personal trainer who will mix things up with new routines for every workout session.

Do you want to be a physically and mentally fit leader? Ask yourself the following questions:

EXERCISING EXERCISE

- How many minutes of exercise do you get each week?

- What is your preferred form of exercise?

- How do you feel after an exercise session?

- What steps are you taking to incorporate regular exercise into your life?

- What keeps you from exercising at least five days a week?

See page 179 for exercise worksheet.

31) Strike a Balance Between Personal and Professional Obligations 32) Calendarize Commitments
33) Overcome Overwhelm **34) Exercise for Lifelong Health** 35) Make Healthier Food Choices 36) Take Time Out
37) Manage Stress 38) Choose Optimism 39) Oscillate Between Periods of Work and Rest 40) Go the Distance

IN THE REAL WORLD

Bringing Back Recess

When we were little kids, most of us led highly active lives. Back then, it was quite natural to spend hours running around the backyard with friends or to break a sweat on the school playground during recess. But somewhere along the line, as we grow older, many of us seem to dedicate less and less time to regular exercise. To make matters worse, the majority of us end up taking on incredibly sedentary jobs, which require very little, if any, physical activity.

For many of us, the lack of exercise really kicks into high gear in the college years. As I started my sophomore year in college, I realized I was spending most of my time sitting around—sitting in the classroom or sitting at the library studying for exams. When I wasn't in class, at the library or in bed sleeping, I was sitting in the dining hall eating lots of starchy foods. It didn't take long before my increase in calories and decrease in activity started to show up in the form of a few extra pounds. This sudden weight gain was enough to drive me to a lifelong commitment to exercise.

As soon as I stepped off the scales, I headed for the indoor track at the school gym. Although the circular track was only about 1/16th of a mile, I was surprised at how much pain I felt as I ran that first lap. My legs were aching and I could feel a burning sensation in my chest as my lungs struggled to expand. To say the least, I was not encouraged by this strenuous experience. But I remembered that old saying, "No pain, no gain," and I pushed through a second lap around the track. When I finished, I decided to come back the next day to see if I could do any better.

Today, several decades later, I can tell you that I successfully conditioned and trained my body in those early days at the gym. I also began what has become a regular exercise habit. For me, starting my day without at least 30 to 45 minutes of exercise is like leaving the house without brushing my teeth. It is a positive habit that drives my confidence and my vitality.

Over the years, I have diversified my exercise routine to keep things interesting. In the early years, I was pretty much addicted to running. I would run or jog three to five miles on a daily basis. (I can tell you that "runners' high" is certainly not a myth—the blast of endorphins you experience after a good run is undeniable.) When I started running, people often asked, "David, why are you always smiling?" It didn't occur to me that I was giving off this joyful expression until more and more people asked me this question. That's when I realized the daily exercise was helping to calibrate my emotional state—and it was apparently showing.

About 10 years ago, I decided to mix up my exercise routine to include more biking, elliptical training, weight lifting and stretching. This added more variety and allowed me to more effectively balance my aerobic and cardiovascular exercises with exercises that focused on resistance and flexibility.

I can't think of a better way to start my day than with a good workout in the gym or in my basement, where I also have some exercise equipment. Whenever I travel, I make sure that my hotel has a decent fitness center, and I always pack my gym shoes and track clothes. This ensures that I'll be able to maintain my regular workout schedule—and it also ensures that my customers, regardless of where they are in the world, get me at my best.

31) Strike a Balance Between Personal and Professional Obligations 32) Calendarize Commitments
33) Overcome Overwhelm 34) Exercise for Lifelong Health **35) Make Healthier Food Choices** 36) Take Time Out
37) Manage Stress 38) Choose Optimism 39) Oscillate Between Periods of Work and Rest 40) Go the Distance

CHAPTER
35

Make Healthier Food Choices

Fit leaders are aware that the foods they eat have an impact on their energy, productivity and mood. During the work day, far too many professionals turn to snacks and drinks filled with excess sugars, salt and other stimulating ingredients in an attempt to give their minds a "boost." On the other hand, a fit leader carefully plans his meals and remains forever mindful, even when he is eating out, about the important relationship between what he eats and how he performs.

In *On Target Living Nutrition* (Chris Johnson, LLC, 2007), author Chris Johnson talks about how we can make simple and often painless "upgrades" when selecting from the many foods available to us. While it's easy to get caught up in an endless cycle of fad diets (each with their own mantra of how much fat, protein and/or carbohydrates should be consumed for best results), Chris says we need to focus more on the quality of the foods we consume.

Most people are unaware of the relative acidity or alkalinity (pH value) of the foods they eat. Foods such as table salt, sugar, soda pop (regular or diet) and many meats produce acid in the body. On the other hand, foods such as sea salt, mineral water, pumpkin seeds, many fruits and vegetables, most spices and green tea produce alkaline in the body.

If you want to make healthier food choices, answer the following questions:

HEALTHY EATING EXERCISE

- How acidic is your diet?

- How much added sugars and salt are you consuming in your diet?

- How much water are you drinking each day?

- How much time do you take to plan your meals and snacks while away from home?

- What three simple upgrades could you make in the next month to increase the amount of alkaline-producing foods in your diet?

See page 180 for exercise worksheet.

Superfoods and You

Once I started exercising in college, I also began to eat healthier. After all, I wanted to make sure my diet didn't reverse all the good that came from my daily workouts. I gradually replaced soda pop with water, coffee with green tea and sweets with nuts and whole grains. I now stay away from overly processed foods, and I eat fewer calories, especially after dinner.

For many years, I thought I was doing everything possible to maintain a healthy diet. Then, several years ago, I was introduced to four different Superfoods that I have since incorporated into my diet. These four whole foods have substantially increased my energy and have contributed to a more alkaline diet.

Here's a breakdown of the four Superfoods I eat every day:

1. Cod Liver Oil

I take one tablespoon of Cod Liver Oil every morning after I drink my breakfast smoothie. I strongly recommend the lemon-flavored version. Some people prefer to blend their daily Cod Liver Oil into salad dressings, which is another great way to incorporate this Superfood into your diet.

Cod Liver Oil is extremely high in Omega 3 fatty acids, which benefit your heart and brain by lowering cholesterol and improving the efficiency of energy production by the mitochondria in your cells.

I purchase my Cod Liver Oil at On Target Living in Bath, Michigan. Since the Cod Liver Oil must be refrigerated after opening, I also purchase this Superfood in capsule form for when I am traveling.

2. Flaxseed

I add one tablespoon of ground flaxseed to my breakfast smoothie every morning. Because all of the nutrition in these seeds is found within the shell, I use a small coffee grinder to produce enough flax meal for a few days and then refrigerate it. If you eat the seeds whole, they will simply pass through your body without releasing their full benefit.

Not only are flaxseeds very high in Omega 3 fatty acids, they also contain lignans, which have antiviral, antifungal, antibacterial and anticancer properties. Flaxseeds decrease inflammation, help lower cholesterol and keep cell walls soft.

I purchase Golden Roasted Flaxseeds at my local Trader Joe's. They are inexpensive, and one bag lasts a while if you refrigerate it.

31) Strike a Balance Between Personal and Professional Obligations 32) Calendarize Commitments
33) Overcome Overwhelm 34) Exercise for Lifelong Health **35) Make Healthier Food Choices** 36) Take Time Out
37) Manage Stress 38) Choose Optimism 39) Oscillate Between Periods of Work and Rest 40) Go the Distance

3. Wheatgrass

I take wheatgrass every morning before my workout. Wheatgrass is available in "ice cube" or tablet form. You can also grow your own wheatgrass or purchase it in powder form. Some people add the powder to smoothies. I personally prefer the ice cubes.

Wheatgrass contains more than 90 different minerals and gives your body a boost of alkalinity. This Superfood is also high in chlorophyll, which aids digestion and elimination of toxic substances.

I purchase my Wheatgrass in ice cube form at On Target Living, and I purchase Wheatgrass tablets from Pines International in Lawrence, Kansas.

4. Spirulina/Chlorella

I take two grams of a spirulina/chlorella blend throughout the course of each day. While it's available as a powder, I prefer taking it in tablet form.

This Superfood contains more chlorophyll and nucleic acids (DNA and RNA) than any other known plant. It is 65 percent protein and highly alkaline. Consisting of 19 amino acids, including all 10 of the essential amino acids (those that must be obtained through the diet), chlorella can be used as a daily body detoxifier.

I purchase my Spirulina/Chlorella from On Target Living in Bath, Michigan.

In addition to the four Superfoods described above, consider adding some or all of the following Superfoods to your diet on a regular basis:

- Blueberries
- Broccoli
- Steel-cut oats
- Oranges
- Pumpkin
- Salmon
- Spinach
- Tea (green or black)
- Tomatoes
- Walnuts
- Kale
- Avocado
- Figs
- Beets
- Apples
- Lemons and Limes

CHAPTER
36

Take Time Out

Fit leaders take time to "do nothing." While inactivity is often frowned upon in our fast-paced society, it's important for a leader to take time out, rest and relax. This downtime allows him to gather his thoughts, gain perspective and relieve stress. In fact, if you want to live a happy and fulfilled life, a certain amount of idleness is essential.

In a rather ironic twist, when you know you can catch up on work during weekends or late evenings, your overall productivity can actually decrease during the rest of the day. That's because you assume if you don't get enough accomplished during the regular work day, you can get it done during the evening or weekend—a time that might be better spent on rejuvenating activities.

If you want to maintain vitality, find a system that protects your ability to rest and rejuvenate—and learn that "doing nothing" is not a selfish act.

Have you mastered the art of rest and relaxation? Ask yourself the following questions:

TIME OUT EXERCISE

- How do you disconnect from the pressures of your job?

- How many hours of sleep do you get on a consistent basis?

- When was the last time you took a real vacation?

- How often do you stop to take a few deep breaths?

- What would it take for you to believe in the restorative power of downtime?

See page 181 for exercise worksheet.

31) Strike a Balance Between Personal and Professional Obligations 32) Calendarize Commitments
33) Overcome Overwhelm 34) Exercise for Lifelong Health 35) Make Healthier Food Choices **36) Take Time Out**
37) Manage Stress 38) Choose Optimism 39) Oscillate Between Periods of Work and Rest 40) Go the Distance

Five Ways to Slow Down

If you want to maintain vitality, it's important to learn how to slow down and take a breather. Here are five simple ways you can rest, relax and recharge:

1. Sleep

Doctors, scientists and researchers are constantly pointing out the unparalleled recuperative powers a good night's sleep provides. According to the National Sleep Foundation, most adults require seven to eight hours of shut eye. Like many busy professionals, I used to think I could get by on just five hours of sleep a night. Given my demanding executive schedule and my morning exercise habit, I decided that was all the time I could afford to dedicate to sleep. However, I didn't realize I was missing out on the full healing effects sleep provides.

When you sleep, especially when you enter that period of sleeping known as rapid eye movement or REM, your body is undergoing a critical cycle of physical, mental and emotional healing. When you don't get enough of these deeper sleep cycle segments (and you don't if you are not sleeping for seven to eight hours a night), you are not reaping the full benefits of one of nature's most powerful elixirs.

I used to make all the excuses in the world for not sleeping more...until I learned exactly what I was compromising. I finally made a personal commitment to sleep for seven to eight hours every night. For me, this means I have to get to bed earlier, since I don't have the option of starting my day any later. These days, I always plan ahead for sleep and I include ample time for winding down. This ensures that I don't replace my sleeping time with other less vital activities, like watching *The Late Show*.

2. Deep Breathing

Most of us inhale and exhale without any conscious awareness of the physical act. Of course, this is typically a good thing. However, I have learned to stop several times each day to become more aware of my breathing. When I do, I often notice that my breaths are too shallow. When I take the time to breathe more deeply, I feel an instant rush of well-being—and any stress I may be experiencing seems to melt away.

You can relax and take a welcome respite from the more frenetic parts of your day by belly breathing, or breathing from your diaphragm as opposed to your chest. Deep breathing also offers an added benefit to your vagus nerve. The vagus nerve (pronounced vay-gus), which extends from your brain stem to the organs in your neck, thorax, and abdomen, carries sensory information from your organs back to your brain. Too much sensory input, often caused by mental or physical stress, can overload your brain, causing it to "short circuit." According to Dr. Michael F. Roizen and Dr. Mehmet C. Oz, authors of "You: Staying Young" (Free Press, 2007), we can help calm the vagus nerve by breathing deeply through our diaphragms and engaging in other forms of relaxation.

3. Progressive Muscle Relaxation

I was introduced to progressive muscle relaxation during my first yoga class. While I personally find yoga postures to be a bit challenging, I have always enjoyed the relaxation period at the end of most yoga sessions.

Here's how it works: Lie down on a mat, or any soft surface, and become aware of your feet and toes. Focus on relaxing that part of your body. Once your feet and toes are fully relaxed (usually after a minute or two), do the same thing for each section of your body all the way up to your head. Relax through the lower portion of your legs, then the upper portion, then the pelvic area followed by the abdomen. Next, relax your chest area, your shoulders and neck and finally your head. By the time you move from the bottom of your body to the very top, you will feel incredibly relaxed.

The first time I practiced this relaxation technique, I was one of about 20 students in a yoga class. I will never forget waking up at the end of class, looking around embarrassed as I realized no one else was in the room. The progressive muscle relaxation was so effective, it put me right to sleep!

As you work through progressive muscle relaxation, it's important to let go and use this time to truly slow down. There are plenty of pressures waiting for you when you return to the world of awareness…so make the most of this short time of rest.

4. Music

Some people prefer to slow down by listening to their favorite music. With so much musical technology available to us these days, from iPods to streaming online music, we can listen to music at the office, at home, in the car, at the gym or practically anywhere else. While some prefer softer forms of musical entertainment, like classical or soft pop, others have more eclectic tastes.

I will often stream music live from my favorite radio station as I write a customer proposal or compose a report. The background music relaxes me and prevents me from tensing up. The tunes also remind me to breathe more

31) Strike a Balance Between Personal and Professional Obligations 32) Calendarize Commitments
33) Overcome Overwhelm 34) Exercise for Lifelong Health 35) Make Healthier Food Choices **36) Take Time Out**
37) Manage Stress 38) Choose Optimism 39) Oscillate Between Periods of Work and Rest 40) Go the Distance

deeply. Music is a great way to loosen up and create more resonance as you move through your busy day.

5. Meditation

When I mention meditation in my leadership workshops, I am often met with blank stares. Although once practiced primarily in the Eastern part of the world, meditation has become much more widespread in recent years. Today, people across the globe use meditation as a way to relax and slow down from the hectic pace of their lives.

There are many forms of meditation. Some methods involve concentration or control of the mind while others involve contemplation. Many years ago, I was personally trained in a form of meditation called TM, or Transcendental Meditation. TM helps your mind simply, naturally and effortlessly transcend thinking, allowing you to experience a deep state of restfully alert consciousness. This method became somewhat famous when The Beatles were trained in TM by the Maharishi Mahesh Yogi.

In the 1970s, a Harvard-trained cardiologist, Herbert Benson, wrote a book called *The Relaxation Response* (HarperTorch, 1976). Based on studies at Boston's Beth Israel Hospital and Harvard Medical School, Dr. Benson showed that relaxation techniques such as meditation have immense physical benefits, from lowered blood pressure to a reduction in heart disease. According to Dr. Benson, anyone can reap the benefits of meditation—with or without a guru's guidance. Dr. Benson has since authored a new book called *The Relaxation Revolution* (Scribner, 2010).

The secret to slowing down is finding a relaxation technique that works for you. Experiment with one or more of these five approaches to rest and recharge.

CHAPTER
37

Manage Stress

Fit leaders know that a certain level of stress can help them stay focused, energetic and alert. However, once stress reaches a certain threshold, it stops being helpful and starts being harmful. In fact, stress can disrupt nearly every system in a person's body.

In 1975, endocrinologist Hans Selye published a model dividing stress into two major categories: eustress and distress. According to Selye, eustress is a positive form of stress that enhances a person's physical or mental function (such as through strength training or challenging work). On the other hand, distress is persistent negative stress that is not resolved through coping or adaptation. This type of stress may lead to anxiety, withdrawal or depression.

When you are under excessive amounts of negative stress, you can experience cognitive, emotional, physical or behavioral effects, including:

- poor judgment
- a general negative outlook
- excessive worrying
- moodiness
- agitation
- nausea, dizziness or rapid heartbeat
- inability to relax
- changes in diet
- nervous habits, such as pacing and nail-biting

If you are exhibiting any of these behaviors, it may be a sign that you're not managing your stress level. Ask yourself the following questions:

STRESS MANAGEMENT EXERCISE

- How do you differentiate between eustress and distress in your life?
- What are the tell-tale signs of distress for you?
- What coping strategies do you employ today to deal with the potentially debilitating impacts of stress?
- How are you managing your workload to avoid burnout?
- When have you experienced a wakeup call that caused you to reevaluate the way you want to live your life and what you want to achieve in your career?

See page 182 for exercise worksheet.

31) Strike a Balance Between Personal and Professional Obligations 32) Calendarize Commitments
33) Overcome Overwhelm 34) Exercise for Lifelong Health 35) Make Healthier Food Choices 36) Take Time Out
37) **Manage Stress** 38) Choose Optimism 39) Oscillate Between Periods of Work and Rest 40) Go the Distance

IN THE REAL WORLD

Under Pressure: How I Conquered Job Stress

Early in my career, I began to notice a trend: As I signed up for more and more responsibilities, I experienced increasing amounts of stress. I started to worry about whether I would be able to deliver on all of my promises as I watched my list of commitments grow longer and longer. Because I was an avid runner, I assumed my daily exercise would serve as protection against my growing stress level.

However, when I moved into my first executive role, I quickly realized that my running habit was simply not enough to inoculate me against the rising stress of my job. As I discussed this one day with a colleague, she suggested that I go float. When you go "floating," you are closed up in a large, light-proof, sound-proof flotation tank filled with a shallow pool of water and Epsom salt, which is five times denser and more buoyant than sea water. This allows you to lie back and float effortlessly on the surface with all parts of your body firmly supported…almost like an astronaut in zero gravity.

At first, I thought my colleague was joking. The idea of spending my lunch hour wearing nothing but a bathing suit, cocooned in a floatation tank, buoyed in total darkness for 60 minutes, seemed a bit on the fringe—even for me.

But I decided to give it a shot, and I spent one hour a week floating for almost six months. It was one of the most peaceful experiences of my life. The salt in the tank permitted me to lie motionless on my back without effort, close my eyes and listen to whatever music I chose for the hour. When I emerged from the tank, I was literally floating. When I returned to the office, everyone knew I had just floated because I was so mellow.

It was clear that I had found the perfect stress reliever. Unfortunately, the float store across the street from my office eventually closed its doors due to lack of business (I guess even flotation tank businesses can sink). I wasn't sure how I was going to replace the serenity I achieved when I escaped into the tank each week.

Interestingly, the same colleague who initially recommended that I float every week went on to recommend an even more powerful form of relaxation, one that has helped me manage my stress ever since. She suggested that I treat myself to a weekly Swedish massage. Admittedly, I was a bit squeamish about getting a massage at first. At the same time, I knew I needed to find a replacement for my weekly floats.

Being the adventurous person I am, I decided to give it a try—and the rest is history. For the past 15 years, I have been seeing the same massage therapist every week. The 60 minutes I spend at her center each week are truly grounding, giving me the opportunity to absorb her healing energy and truly relax. While a weekly massage may seem a bit extravagant, I remember reading that Bob Hope received a daily massage—and Bob lived to be 100.

Whether you seek out floating, a regular massage or some other form of relaxation, it is critical to find some way to regulate your stress. After all, stress management is an essential part of a healthy and vital life. Relaxation isn't just about peace of mind. It is also a process that decreases the wear and tear on your mind and body from the challenges and hassles of daily life.

31) Strike a Balance Between Personal and Professional Obligations 32) Calendarize Commitments
33) Overcome Overwhelm 34) Exercise for Lifelong Health 35) Make Healthier Food Choices 36) Take Time Out
37) Manage Stress **38) Choose Optimism** 39) Oscillate Between Periods of Work and Rest 40) Go the Distance

CHAPTER
38

Choose Optimism

Fit leaders are optimistic and always try to see the glass as half-full. When a leader chooses optimism, he also chooses vitality and success.

Martin E.P. Seligman, a former President of the American Psychological Association and a pioneer in the field of positive psychology, has been studying optimists and pessimists for 25 years. In his national bestseller *Learned Optimism* (Pocket Books, 1990, 1998) Seligman writes that pessimists react to setbacks with "a presumption of personal helplessness." Pessimists believe that bad events will last a long time and are somehow their fault.

On the other hand, optimists react to setbacks from "a presumption of personal power," according to Seligman. They view bad events as temporary setbacks that are isolated to particular circumstances. Optimists believe they can overcome bad events through their effort and abilities.

The way you define your circumstances determines whether you are optimistic or pessimistic. When you choose optimism, you inoculate yourself against the feeling of helplessness and strengthen your emotional competence, which leads to increased productivity.

Are you an optimist or a pessimist? Ask yourself the following questions:

OPTIMISM EXERCISE

- When something doesn't work out for you, to what do you attribute the outcome?

- How much time do you spend complaining about how nothing works the way it should?

- What is it like for you to be around pessimists?

- How can you change your perspective to see the glass as half full versus half empty?

- How does choosing optimism increase your confidence, effectiveness and vitality?

See page 183 for exercise worksheet.

Is The Glass Half Empty or Half Full?

As you answered the Optimism Exercise questions on the previous page, you might have come to terms with the fact that you are a bona fide pessimist. Not to worry. As Seligman points out, optimism is a learned behavior. In other words, even if you have a habit of seeing the glass as half empty, you can teach yourself to look on the bright side.

Here are five simple tips that will get you on the road to optimism:

1. Know that most bad things are not permanent.

When something goes wrong, try not to blow things out of proportion. Ask yourself if the negative effect is permanent. More often than not, it's only temporary. Optimists realize that most bad events are fleeting and will not permanently alter the course of their lives.

2. Give yourself credit for positive events.

When something good happens, take time to pat yourself on the back. Celebrate your strengths and think about the ways you contributed (both directly and indirectly) to this accomplishment.

3. Cut yourself some slack.

Pessimists often blame themselves for every negative event. But when things don't go as planned, it's not always your fault. Consider the extenuating circumstances that could have contributed to the bad outcome. Not every failure is caused by one of your own personal weaknesses.

4. Remember there's always next time.

Instead of dwelling on your mistakes, try to think about how you can do better next time. When you start to embrace failures as powerful learning experiences, you're beginning to think more like an optimist.

5. Challenge your negative thoughts.

When you catch yourself thinking negatively, stop, take a deep breath and make a conscious effort to change your thought pattern. The more often you challenge negative thoughts, the more natural it will become for you to think like an optimist. Before you know it, you'll be finding the positive in almost any situation.

31) Strike a Balance Between Personal and Professional Obligations 32) Calendarize Commitments
33) Overcome Overwhelm 34) Exercise for Lifelong Health 35) Make Healthier Food Choices 36) Take Time Out
37) Manage Stress 38) Choose Optimism **39) Oscillate Between Periods of Work and Rest** 40) Go the Distance

CHAPTER
39

Oscillate Between Periods of Work and Rest

Fit leaders inject vitality into their lives by alternating between periods of high energy expenditure and periods of rest and recovery. A successful leader knows how to balance competing demands for her time by oscillating between work and play.

Dan Sullivan, creator of The Strategic Coach® Program, and Jennifer White, author of *Work Less, Make More* (Wiley, 1999), discuss how important it is for professionals to take time to rest and recover. Both Sullivan and White say that each week, professionals need to carve out "Free Days" devoted exclusively to rejuvenation.

When you take a Free Day, you don't do any work—which also means no business-related email or voicemail. You spend a full 24 hours focusing only on recreation and relaxation. Vital to everyone's life, Free Days are for hobbies, family, exercise and reflection. These are the days when you disconnect completely from work and take time to recuperate from the daily demands of your job.

How well do you oscillate between periods of work and rest? Ask yourself the following questions:

ENERGY VS. RECOVERY EXERCISE

- How many Free Days have you taken during the last 90 days?

- How do your Free Days enhance your overall leadership effectiveness and vitality?

- What activities do you find truly rejuvenating?

- What does it take for you to disconnect from your work?

- How comfortable are you saying yes to yourself?

See page 184 for exercise worksheet.

Paving the Way for Free Days

As leaders seek to lead an "oscillating" life, one of the vexing challenges they face is figuring out what to do on a Free Day. When you have created a routine of working all the time, it can be difficult to imagine how else you could possibly spend your days.

If you're struggling to figure out how to spend your Free Days, here are a few suggestions:

- Go for a jog or a long walk
- Meditate
- Get a massage
- Read a book
- Go to a movie
- Watch your favorite DVDs
- Listen to music
- Write letters (the old-fashioned way)
- Go to lunch with a friend
- Take your kids to the park
- Go on a "date" with your significant other

Once you've figured out how to spend your Free Days, the true challenge is keeping your commitment to taking them on a consistent basis. Here are a few ways to increase the likelihood that you will actually follow through with Free Days:

Calendarize Free Days

Plan ahead by designating specific days on your calendar for rejuvenation. Mark these days as full-day appointments with yourself.

Pave the way

Take the necessary steps to clear the path for your Free Days. You can do this by completing or deferring other work that could get in your way of getting away.

Let others know

Make sure your family, coworkers and others around you understand your commitment to Free Days, and ask them for their support.

31) Strike a Balance Between Personal and Professional Obligations 32) Calendarize Commitments
33) Overcome Overwhelm 34) Exercise for Lifelong Health 35) Make Healthier Food Choices 36) Take Time Out
37) Manage Stress 38) Choose Optimism **39) Oscillate Between Periods of Work and Rest** 40) Go the Distance

Focus on all of your energy sources

When planning your Free Days, try to plan activities that enhance all four of your energy sources: physical, emotional, mental and spiritual.

Learn to say yes to yourself

Get comfortable making time for yourself. The oscillation you build into your life will significantly enhance your clarity, confidence, effectiveness and vitality.

CHAPTER
40

Go the Distance

Fit leaders create sustainable impact when they successfully integrate all four faces of leadership fitness: clarity, confidence, effectiveness and vitality. When a leader pursues activities that enhance his personal health and vibrancy, he develops incredible stamina. Therefore, a leader who adds vitality to his repertoire is more likely to go the distance.

Leaders who lack vitality and stamina run out of steam far too early in their careers. They eventually hit a wall and discover they do not have the energy to move forward.

If you want to be a fit leader, it's important to embrace the interrelationships among all four dynamic qualities of leadership fitness: clarity, confidence, effectiveness and vitality. I have found that the synergies between vitality and the other three leadership fitness components often outweigh the synergies between any of the other qualities in our model:

- With vitality, it is easier to achieve clarity.
- With vitality, it is more likely that leaders will remain confident.
- With vitality, leaders have the energy it takes to lead and manage effectively.

In other words, without vitality, you will not have the endurance to go the distance. Ask yourself the following questions:

STAMINA EXERCISE

- What keeps you from going the distance?

- How will an increase in your vitality impact your clarity?

- How will an increase in your vitality impact your confidence?

- How will an increase in your vitality impact your effectiveness?

- What three steps will you take in the next 90 days to increase your vitality?

See page 185 for exercise worksheet.

31) Strike a Balance Between Personal and Professional Obligations 32) Calendarize Commitments
33) Overcome Overwhelm 34) Exercise for Lifelong Health 35) Make Healthier Food Choices 36) Take Time Out
37) Manage Stress 38) Choose Optimism 39) Oscillate Between Periods of Work and Rest **40) Go the Distance**

IN THE REAL WORLD

The 90-Day Runway

Leaders who go the distance make a lifelong commitment to the continuous development of positive habits. In my own life, I am most successful when I set and achieve 90-day goals. I have found that a single calendar quarter provides just the right amount of time and space for me to shift my thinking and behavior.

If you spend some time online or peruse the business and personal development shelves of any local bookstore, you likely will find numerous titles and references pointing to the significance of "the next 90 days." When I recently did a quick Internet search for the phrase "next 90 days," my search engine uncovered the following results:

- Surviving the Next 90 Days
- The 90-Day Health Challenge
- Make $100,000 in the Next 90 Days
- Your First 90 Days on the Job
- 90 Days to a New Life Direction
- Making an Impact in the First 90 Days

While some might argue there's nothing magical about the 90-day period, the important point is this: When you adopt a meaningful framework or perspective (such as a 90-day timeframe), it can help you plan for the future results you desire. After all, the plans you put in motion today surely will have an impact on where you end up in the future. If you're like most leaders, a 90-day period creates a sufficient runway for you to achieve meaningful progress toward your goals.

Over the course of our year-long Institute for Leadership Fitness, we introduce numerous new tools and processes, each providing leaders with a fresh opportunity to shift their thinking and behaviors. We break the year-long program into four 90-day periods to monitor each leader's progress in achieving greater clarity, confidence, effectiveness and vitality. These four 90-day periods have proven to be extremely successful for the leaders we train.

As you work to close the gap between where you are today and where you want to be in the future, it might be helpful to consult *The Path of Least Resistance for Managers* (Berrett-Koehler Publishers, 1999) by Robert Fritz, who introduces the concept of structural tension. According to Fritz, once leaders determine their desired result and can juxtapose that with their current reality, they have created tension that can only be resolved by reducing the distance between current reality and desired state.

In his own words, Fritz writes:

"I can't say this strongly enough. This principle of structural tension—knowing what we want to create and knowing where we are in relationship to our goals—is the most powerful force an organization can have.

"But it can sound too simple—and in a way it is too simple. Too simple to say, too simple to hear, so simple that it's easy to dismiss it, underestimate it, not quite get it, but think that we've gotten it.

"It is easy to say: know what we want, know where we are, and develop a plan to get from here to there. But the actuality is hard, very hard."

As a leader, your ultimate goal is to reduce the distance between today's reality and the outcomes you and your organization desire. When you create space for making the necessary shifts in your thinking and behavior, you can go the distance—and become a fit leader for life.

EXERCISES

PART 1

CLARITY:

[Exercises]

Setting Expectations Exercise

What behaviors and actions do you expect of your team?

How well does your team understand what is expected of them?

How can you more clearly define your expectations for your employees?

How much time have you spent communicating your expectations to your staff?

How could providing a written list of expectations to your team help them stay on track?

Removing Ambiguity Exercise

How well does your team understand the direction you've set for the organization?

What questions would you ask yourself to gain more clarity?

How many times and how many different ways do you communicate
an important message to your team?

How much time and productivity have you lost in the past by being less than clear?

What are the visible signs that others truly understand your message?

Reflection Exercise

How much time do you spend really pondering your possibilities?

What processes do you employ to sufficiently consider alternatives?

When have you caught yourself rushing to action prematurely?

How much free space exists in your weekly schedule?

How do you avoid analysis paralysis?

Understanding Your Customers Exercise

How much time are you spending with your key customers?

What process does your organization use to share customer needs and concerns with the team members who need to know them?

What are the top three business issues keeping your customers up at night?

How does your organization track customer issues to create a sense of urgency around your company's agenda?

How are you nurturing your key customer relationships?

Focus Exercise

What must your team achieve in the next 90 days to move your strategy forward?

What is currently distracting you from your focus on your objectives?

What short-cuts are you tempted to take in an attempt to reach your goal more quickly?

How tightly are you holding on to positions that no longer make sense
or are no longer the best approach?

What is the source of your clarity in the course you've charted?

Open-Ended Questions Exercise

How aware are you of the types of questions you ask every day?

What is the risk of relying on closed-ended questions to get the information you seek?

How can you replace closed-ended questions, that often serve as poorly disguised statements of your own position, with powerful open-ended questions?

What would it be like to spend an entire meeting asking only open-ended questions?

When is it appropriate to ask a closed-ended question?

Meaningful Conversations Exercise

What are you doing today to create an environment of trust and mutual respect?

How are you encouraging all members of your team to share their unique points of view?

What is your practice around the use of electronic devices during one-on-one and group meetings?

What impact would your commitment to having regular conversations have on overall employee engagement?

How do you remain present when interacting with others?

Rounding Exercise

How much time do you currently spend just walking around the office?

How much time will you devote to rounding in your organization?

What types of information are more likely to emerge from a more casual encounter with staff?

What times of the day, week and the month are the most suitable for you to make rounds?

What would the value be to you if other members of your team were to round, as well?

Mission, Vision and Values Exercise

What is the core purpose of your organization?

How would you describe your team's contribution to the overall mission of the organization?

What is the "why" of your organization that inspires others to go there with you?

What organizational or team values drive the culture of your workforce?

What is the gap between the values you currently see in your organization
and the values you desire to see?

Prioritizing Opportunities Exercise

What are the key opportunities your organization could decide to pursue over the course of the next 12 months?

What key opportunities are "in the bullseye" for your organization based upon market need and organizational strategy?

What key opportunities would you pursue only on an opportunistic basis?

How do you avoid becoming distracted by opportunities that simply remove your focus from what's most important?

How do you communicate your priorities on a regular basis to focus your team's efforts?

PART 2

CONFIDENCE

[Exercises]

Gremlins Exercise

What negative inner voices are you hearing?

What strategies do you use to manage self-doubt?

What thoughts and behaviors feed your confidence despite the critical noise all around you?

What's the worst thing that has happened to you when you moved forward with an idea or program you felt strongly about, despite the presence of nagging doubts?

When have you been swayed by others to stop pursuing something you knew was right?

Powerful Intentions Exercise

How high are you setting the bar for your people?

What is holding you back from going after even more?

Where might you be setting your sights too low?

How do you leverage the power of intention?

What is the boldest intention you've set in the last six months?

Convincing Others to Follow Exercise

What contributes to your success when it comes to winning people over?

How often do you bury your audience in piles of numbers and analyses and lose the opportunity to connect your ideas to real results?

How often do you interpret an objection as a "no" rather than as a signal that your audience simply needs more information?

How consistently do you adapt your presentation to your audience's unique communication preferences?

How effectively do you follow up "after the sale"?

Curiosity Exercise

How do you demonstrate your genuine curiosity and interest in others' thoughts and ideas?

What is your public response when members of your team shoot down others' ideas before attempting to understand them?

What impact will you have on your team if you choose to be furious (disagree first, ask questions later) instead of curious?

How can curiosity advance and encourage your team's learning process?

What is the benefit of being curious even when you know the answers to your questions?

Empowerment Exercise

How do you ignite a spark that compels others to get behind your ideas?

What gets in the way of your people getting on board with your program?

How do your energize your team?

What does empowerment look and feel like to you?

What empowers you?

Positive Feedback Exercise

How often do you provide positive feedback to members of your team?

What impact does your praise have on overall employee confidence and engagement?

How do you keep track of the positive accomplishments of your people?

What is your ratio of positive to constructive feedback?

What other approaches do you take to build up the confidence of your staff?

Trust Exercise

How often do you micromanage others?

How do you instill confidence in your team members?

How do you remind yourself to let others complete the projects you have assigned to them?

How do you stay focused on the big picture?

What successes have you had when you trusted others to do their jobs?

Rewarding Exercise

What personally motivates you to excel?

How are you respecting your team members' need for autonomy?

What is the "why" behind the goals and activities of your organization?

In what areas of their work do your people have opportunities to achieve mastery?

How long-lasting are the effects of some of the more traditional "carrot and stick" rewards you have used in the past?

Embracing Failure Exercise

What actions do you take to promote risk taking in your organization?

What actions do you take that might discourage risk taking?

What happens when someone in your organization takes a risk and fails?

Where have you failed in the last twelve months?

How is the fear of failure holding you back?

Positive Habits Exercise

What positive habits feed your confidence?

What reminders or structures do you employ to maintain a positive focus?

How long does it take you to establish a new pattern of behavior?

What personal practices embolden you on a daily basis?

What can you do to get out of your own way?

PART 3

EFFECTIVENESS

Exercises

Establishing Objectives Exercise

What is the mix of Results, Relationship and Renewal objectives
you have set for individuals on your team?

What are some examples of Relationship objectives you might establish
for members of your team?

How many times throughout the year do you sit down to review progress
against goals and objectives?

What objectives have you set in the past year that stretched the capabilities of your team?

How inspiring are the goals and objectives in your organization?

Delegation Exercise

What stands in your way of delegating more?

How long is your "short list" of people you go to on a routine basis to get things done?

How deep is your bench of talented leaders ready to take on more senior-level assignments?

What projects are you currently working on that can be delegated to others?

What important work is not receiving your attention because of your continued involvement with work that can be handled by others?

Healthy Conflict Exercise

How do you encourage powerful discussion and debate during team meetings?

How consensual are you?

What do you do to avoid becoming defensive when confronting objections to your plans?

What techniques do you use to encourage participation by everyone during a meeting?

How do you keep track of the different possibilities generated by your team?

Feedback Exercise

When was the last time you offered positive feedback to an employee?

When you choose not to provide feedback to others, who steps in to do this for you?

How do you utilize positive and constructive feedback to develop team members?

When providing feedback, how important is it to address how the employee's behavior is impacting your team, the organization and customers?

How do you follow-up with employees after you've given them feedback?

Future Results Exercise

How likely is it that this executive will succeed in the new environment?

What kind of disruption might you cause by bringing someone in from the outside?

What type of assimilation coaching will you provide to ease his transition?

What are your true motives for wanting a former colleague to join you in this new organization?

How long can you wait for this executive to get up to speed?

Accountability Exercise

What is your track record when it comes to honoring your promises and commitments to others?

How do you hold members of your team accountable for their commitments?

When have you chosen excuses, whining or playing the victim instead of accountability?

Where have you personally taken initiative in the last 90 days?

What will you hold yourself and your team accountable for in the next 90 days?

Complacency Exercise

How wed are you to the status quo?

What information do you share with your team to keep them aware
of both dangers and opportunities?

How do you factor objective feedback into your decision making and planning process?

How often do you use "happy talk" when communicating organizational challenges?

What are you doing to defeat complacency in your organization?

Effective Communication Exercise

What are the different ways that you communicate with your team?

How do you know when your communication is ineffective?

What types of communication do you prefer from others?

How do you communicate team priorities in a way that aligns people with what is most important to them and the organization?

How do you ensure that your communication is timely?

Active Listening Exercise

How do you feel when someone else is not truly listening to you?

How often do you catch yourself rushing to formulate your next response while the other person is still speaking?

How will the quality of your relationships be affected by more active listening on your part?

What will it take for you to finish listening before you begin speaking?

How will you change your personal listening experience to make it more fulfilling?

Leader Development Exercise

Who are your high-performing employees?

What process do you have in place to regularly review the talent in your organization?

What are you doing to retain your best people?

What positions on your team are crucial to achieving your current and future business goals?

What legacy do you seek to leave?

PART 4

VITALITY

[Exercises]

Life Balance Exercise

How satisfied are you with the balance in your life today?

What areas of your life would benefit from greater attention?

How often do you truly disconnect from your work?

What is the one small step you might take this week to bring your life more into balance?

How will you boost your balance in the next 90 days?

Calendarizing Exercise

How long is your to-do list?

What are the typical tasks you accumulate each day that can reasonably be completed in two minutes or less?

What tasks are you holding onto that could safely be handled by others?

How many times have you approached the deadline for a task for which you have not scheduled sufficient time to complete?

How often do others in your organization place meetings on your calendar because your calendar shows open space when in fact you need to spend that time working on other commitments?

Overwhelm Exercise

On a scale of 1 to 10, with 10 being the highest, what is your present level of overwhelm?

What are you doing to regain more control over your circumstances?

How much time do you set aside on a weekly basis to plan what needs to get done?

How can you leverage the skills and talents of others to complete your work?

What can you do to avoid the frustration and sense of desperation that arises from having too much to do?

Exercising Exercise

How many minutes of exercise do you get each week?

What is your preferred form of exercise?

How do you feel after an exercise session?

What steps are you taking to incorporate regular exercise into your life?

What keeps you from exercising at least five days a week?

Healthy Eating Exercise

How acidic is your diet?

How much added sugars and salt are you consuming in your diet?

How much water are you drinking each day?

How much time are you taking to plan your meals and snacks while away from home?

What three simple upgrades could you make in the next month to increase the amount of alkaline-producing foods in your diet?

Time Out Exercise

How do you disconnect from the pressures of your job?

How many hours of sleep do you get on a consistent basis?

When was the last time you took a real vacation?

How often do you stop to take a few deep breaths?

What would it take for you to believe in the restorative power of downtime?

Stress Management Exercise

How do you differentiate between eustress and distress in your life?

What are the tell-tale signs of distress for you?

What coping strategies do you employ today to deal with the potentially debilitating impacts of stress?

How are you managing your workload to avoid burnout?

When have you experienced a wakeup call that caused you to reevaluate the way you want to live your life and what you want to achieve in your career?

Optimism Exercise

When something doesn't work out for you, to what do you attribute the outcome?

How much time do you spend complaining about how nothing works the way it should?

What is it like for you to be around pessimists?

How can you change your perspective to see the glass as half full versus half empty?

How does choosing optimism increase your confidence, effectiveness and vitality?

Energy vs. Recovery Exercise

How many Free Days have you taken during the last 90 days?

How do your Free Days enhance your overall leadership effectiveness and vitality?

What activities do you find truly rejuvenating?

What does it take for you to disconnect from your work?

How comfortable are you saying yes to yourself?

Stamina Exercise

What keeps you from going the distance?

How will an increase in your vitality impact your clarity?

How will an increase in your vitality impact your confidence?

How will an increase in your vitality impact your effectiveness?

What three steps will you take in the next 90 days to increase your vitality?